ENDORS

This is a timely book. There is no doubt that we are in the beginning of one of the greatest harvest of souls in our lifetime; and perhaps the end-time harvest as well.

Joe Oden's book, *The Lightnings of God*, gives you a user-friendly, easy-to-read, road map on how to be a part of this. I guarantee that this book is anything but boring, and will change your life!

CINDY JACOBS
Generals International

Joe Oden is the real deal. I have watched his life and ministry for well over 20 years, and he is a true evangelist, grounded in the Word, empowered by the Spirit, and with a burning heart for the lost. Now, in this practical, life-changing book, Joe helps equip you to do the work of evangelism in the fullness of the Spirit. Is there anything more important we can do than win souls for the Lord?

DR. MICHAEL L. BROWN
President, FIRE School of Ministry, and
host of *the Line of Fire* radio broadcast

Joe Oden is a mighty firebrand raised up for such a time as this. He is part prophet, part evangelist, and ALL revival-ist. I have gotten the privilege of hanging around him and the radical rub-off is REAL. His message contained within this man-uscript is sure to launch you into a new level of a ballistic Book of

Acts-mantled Christianity. You will be challenged to press into the more and not settle for the less. Your NEW normal is being called out!

Sean Smith

@revseansmith

Author of *Prophetic Evangelism* and *I Am Your Sign*

www.seansmithministries.com

When I first met Joe Oden I noticed a love for the presence of Jesus and a desire to win souls. God is raising up young leaders who love Him and long to introduce others to His beauty. I pray this book will spark the same in your heart as you read it.

Michael Koulianos

Jesus Image

jesusimage.tv

Joe Oden has been my dear friend for many years and I have never ceased to be inspired and challenged by how He lives out the very words of this book. Get ready to be rocked by the incredible stories of God demonstrating His willingness, love, and power to save the lost!

There are many people who talk about evangelism. There are even some who preach about it. Then there are those who actually practice evangelism. Joe Oden is one of those who lives a life of demonstration and love for the lost. His example has inspired and challenged me for years. My prayer is that the words of this book would change your view of evangelism and spur you to action!

Joel Stockstill

There will be a personal and deep atmospheric shift that will take place when you read this powerful new book, *The Lightnings of God,* by my dear friend evangelist/author Joe Oden. This book will awaken you to the fact that we serve a God who can not only do the impossible, but will use those who are wholly committed for His glory. Prepare yourself as you read not only for deep encounters, but an even deeper burden to rescue the lost to arise in your heart. Evangelist Joe reminds us that we must do as Jude 1:22-23 says, *"Be merciful to those who doubt; save others by snatching them from the fire; to others show mercy, mixed with fear—hating even the clothing stained by corrupted flesh* (NIV)." I must warn you, this book could cause you to abandon all and pursue the high call!

PAT SCHATZLINE
Evangelist & Author
Remnant Ministries International

I was transformed because of an encounter with Jesus. That moment altered the entire trajectory of my life. Needless to say, I am a believer in the *Lightning of God.* This generation needs more than scripted words, they need to see and experience the power of God. This book is a call to those willing to be used of God to bring heaven to earth and demonstrate the Gospel. Proceed with caution! This book will challenge your status quo and ignite a fire not easily tamed.

DANIEL K NORRIS
Pastor, Grace World Outreach Church
Evangelist, Daniel K Norris Ministries
Author of *Trail Of Fire* and *Receptivity*

Joe Oden is one of the few true evangelists that I know today. His genuine love for people mixed with the power of the Holy Spirit is a one-two punch that people are unable to resist. I have been with Joe on numerous occasions and watched him minister seamlessly to waiters and waitresses with love and power. Let this book inspire and equip you for those who are hurting.

RICHARD CRISCO
Pastor, Rochester Christian Church

When you're involved in ministry for 50 years, you learn to spot the "real deal!" Joe Oden is just that and his new book captures his passion to impart it to you. Buckle your seatbelt and be prepared to be equipped, inspired and ignited to move in the miraculous as you share the transformative message of the Gospel effectively and powerfully.

LARRY TOMCZAK
Best-selling author and cultural commentator

A book has strong credibility when its author is living out the principles he is writing about. This can be said of Joe Oden and his book, *The Lightnings of God.* Joe is a soul winner and his passion for the lost is contagious when you are around him, and when you read his book.

DOUG CLAY
General Superintendent of the Assemblies of God

I always appreciate when a minister allows the Holy Spirit's power to flow. God can do so much more with just one touch than we can do with a lifetime of preaching or teaching. This is why I love Joe Oden, and why I am glad you're about to read this book. Joe reminds us that it is not by words of human wisdom, but by the power of the Holy Spirit that people are saved and transformed!

RICK DUBOSE
Assistant General Superintendent of the Assemblies of God

THE
LIGHTNINGS
OF GOD

THE LIGHTNINGS OF GOD

HOW TO BE A TRANSMITTER FOR THE POWER OF GOD

JOE ODEN

DESTINY IMAGE® PUBLISHERS, INC.

P.O. Box 310, Shippensburg, PA 17257-0310

"Promoting Inspired Lives."

This book and all other Destiny Image and Destiny Image Fiction books are available at Christian bookstores and distributors worldwide.

Cover design by Eileen Rockwell

Interior design by Terry Clifton

For more information on foreign distributors, call 717-532-3040.

Reach us on the Internet: www.destinyimage.com.

ISBN 13 TP: 978-0-7684-5355-3

ISBN 13 eBook: 978-0-7684-5356-0

ISBN 13 HC: 978-0-7684-5358-4

ISBN 13 LP: 978-0-7684-5357-7

For Worldwide Distribution, Printed in the U.S.A.

2 3 4 5 6 7 8 / 24 23 22 21 20

CONTENTS

FOREWORD

When I was in Lusaka, Zambia for a recent Gospel campaign, the top bishop in the region approached me on the platform during one of the services. What he said was quite profound and revealing. He said, "This week I have had a revelation. We have valued the apostles, prophets, pastors, and teachers, but we have neglected the gift of the evangelist. What I have witnessed on this platform this week has shown me that we need the gift of the evangelist more than ever."

My mentor, Evangelist Reinhard Bonnke, told me that when he was in Bible college, the title of "evangelist" was conferred on someone who failed their theological exams and could not be ordained as a pastor. To these Bible school leaders, an evangelist was literally a failed pastor. But this misunderstanding of the evangelistic gift is changing in our day.

When one looks back through church history it is easy to see the way in which God has progressively restored different gifts, offices, truths, and emphases to the body of Christ. In modern times we have seen great restoration come to the offices of the apostles, prophets, pastors, and teachers. I believe that one of the things that God is doing right now is restoring the unique gift and grace of the evangelist to the church. The results of this restoration will be historic!

Ephesians 4:12 says that the five-fold gifts of ministry have been given to "equip the saints for the work of ministry." True evangelists have a heavenly assignment, not only to evangelize but to equip the body to do the same. The divine pattern established from the beginning is that each would "reproduce after its own kind." This is both a natural and spiritual law. As the saying goes, "You teach what you know, but you reproduce what you are." One of the great benefits of the restoration of the evangelistic gifting in our time will be the explosion of evangelism throughout the church—not only in the pulpits but in the pews as well.

That is why I am so excited about *The Lightnings of God* by my dear friend Joe Oden. It is more than a book; it is an impartation, a gift to the body, from a true evangelist. Joe walks what he talks and has done so for many years. He has trained many hundreds of evangelists one on one and now, through this book, may tens of thousands of Holy Spirit-empowered evangelists arise to reap the greatest harvest in history before Jesus returns.

Evangelist DANIEL KOLENDA
President and CEO Christ for all Nations

Chapter 1

HIGHLY INTOXICATED

As I fled the police one Friday night, highly intoxicated and high on drugs, in a residential neighborhood driving over 70 miles per hour down a dead-end street, I knew the night was not going to end well. This was a picture of my life in a nutshell. How did I get so out of control? Jail time was already hanging over my head from a drug charge and now this. What was I going to do?

Years earlier, my life took a 90-degree turn. At the age of 15, I smoked pot for the first time and liked it. Little did I know this one step would dramatically alter the next few years of my life. My experimentation with pot led to alcoholism and full-on drug addiction shortly thereafter. Within just a few years, I was using just about any drug I could get my hands on and stayed high all the time. Before I knew what hit me, I was a drug addict. My life consisted of getting high, drinking, and selling drugs.

One night I apparently overdosed on LSD. I was out with some friends and asked them to take me home because my back was wrenched and I found myself curled up in a fetal position in my friend's car. I later learned that sometimes a chemical called strychnine is found mixed with "street" drugs such as LSD, heroin, and cocaine. Strychnine is primarily used to kill rats by destroying their nervous system. You usually find them curled up in a fetal position after taking this. I feel that this was happening to me.

At that time, I was still a teenager living with my parents. When I got home, I turned the television to an unusual Christian station called TBN (Trinity Broadcasting Network). The first thing I saw was a long curly-haired man pointing his finger at the camera saying, *"There are some young people watching this program right now and you're hooked on drugs. Not only are you hooked on drugs, but you are in a deep, dark cave of drug addiction. But Jesus Christ is in the cave with you! Not only is He in the cave with you, but He is going to bring you out of the cave. Not only is He going to bring you out, but He is going to set you free and you are going to preach the Gospel around America!"* When he said that, the power of God hit me and I was instantaneously sobered from the LSD overdose. This was a real sign and wonder from God because out of every drug you can take, LSD isn't one that will just instantly end. A trip on LSD lasts between 8–12 hours, and those last hours are a very slow fade of coming back to normal. I began to weep under the power of God and knew God was calling me to serve Him and preach the Gospel, even as a complete heathen. This is God's true grace—though we are not looking for Him, He is looking for us.

I'd love to say that I got down on my knees that night and gave my heart to Christ, but that didn't happen. However, it began a process. In First Corinthians, what Paul described happened to me: *"I planted the seed, Apollos watered it, but God has been making it grow"* (1 Cor. 3:6). Many in the body of Christ don't get saved the first time they hear the Gospel or have an encounter with Christ. As in my case, a seed is planted, but it needs to be cultivated and watered.

After my encounter that night, I began to pray before bed that God would somehow get me into church. I didn't know exactly how to pray, but I knew that if I could get into church I would have a shot at getting set free from drugs. When I was high at parties, I began telling people that I would one day soon preach the Gospel around America. Imagine that! I'm at a party on drugs, and possibly selling them, telling everyone I was going to preach the Gospel soon. I was prophetically speaking out my destiny as a complete sinner. Isn't God gracious and good? A good friend of mine would tell me, "Joe, please don't tell anyone tonight at the party you are going to start preaching the Gospel; it's really embarrassing."

Even though God was calling me, I was headed in the wrong direction harder and faster than ever. LSD, marijuana, crack, alcohol—if I wasn't high, I was trying to get high. All this time, my parents were broken and I wouldn't listen to anyone.

One night after turning 18, I was in Gulf Shores, Alabama on spring break. We had been drinking and smoking dope all day. On our drive to where we were staying, I shot the bird to what appeared to be an undercover police officer or someone who worked with the police department. We both pulled over and I got out of the car with a beer bottle ready to have an altercation with one of them. Then all of a sudden, several police officers showed up out of nowhere. I was highly intoxicated and in possession of drugs, so I went straight to jail. My parents were devastated, I was in trouble with the law, but nothing slowed my descent fueled by drugs.

The judge ordered me to church!

When I was set to go to court, I showed up high. The judge was strict and made me take random drug tests while on probation. I managed to beat several of the tests using crazy methods, but one day it failed and I went to jail. He let me out not long after, but I still didn't slow down. I failed a second drug test, so the judge put me in jail for a year. He wanted to give me *one more* good scare. He ended up letting me out after about 10 days. During my next appearance before him, he warned me sternly that if I messed up any more he would seriously put me in jail for one year with no questions asked. Then he ordered me to go to church every Sunday and get the bulletin signed by the pastor, among other things. Wow! He ordered me to church! God had answered the prayer of this drug-dealing reprobate. Romans 5:10 tells us, *"For if, while we were God's enemies, we were reconciled to him through the death of his Son, how much more, having been reconciled, shall we be saved through his life!"* This judge's ruling was a manifestation of God's grace in a powerful way. I probably could've made the news reporting this to the ACLU because I don't think he had the authority to do this—send someone to church with the consequence of jail time if he doesn't attend. But thank You, Jesus, that he did!

I found a small Assemblies of God church in southern Alabama that a friend visited and told me about. After the first service, I asked the pastor if I could speak with him for a moment. This was an awkward conversation for me to have with him, but I informed him that I had been court-ordered by the law to attend church and I needed him to sign my bulletin every Sunday or I would have to go to jail for a year. I let him know that I had been a drug addict and was arrested for drugs. I would stay out late most Saturday nights, so I attended church every Sunday night.

After six months of church attendance, I walked in one particular night and the atmosphere was completely different. I didn't have a way to articulate what was happening, but I knew God was in the room. I was having visions of the things of God and had not taken any drugs that day. They were having a guest minister from the Brownsville Revival this particular night. The Brownsville Revival had been going on for about two years at this point with thousands of people getting saved every week. The guest minister from the revival was Bob Gladstone. He served as one of the professors at the school birthed out of the revival, called the Brownsville Revival School of Ministry. As he took the stage and began to preach, there was something on him that I had never witnessed on any other preacher. The easiest way to describe it was that God Himself was on this man. With every word he said, I was drawn closer and closer to God. I had heard people get up and speak, but never with the fire that was on this man. He gave a call for all who did not know God to come at once! He said to run to the altar, so I did! I fell on my knees and began to ask God to forgive me of every sin that I could remember that I had ever committed. For the first time in my life, I stood up washed in the blood of Jesus Christ, cleansed of my sins. I knelt down a sinner and I stood up saved.

The minister began to pray for people and walked over to where I was standing. I was the first person he was going to pray for. He asked me what I needed from the Lord. I said, "I'd like to be filled with the Holy Ghost." I did not understand exactly what that meant, but He said, "Okay," and laid his hands on me. The next thing I knew, I was flying back under the power of God and hit the ground. Now, nothing like *this* had ever happened to me before. I wasn't for or against this kind of manifestation, but the only time I fell down was when I had too much to drink—not after someone prayed for me. It just didn't happen in our church or anywhere I had ever been. When I hit the ground I thought to myself, "This feels like I smoked a good joint." I didn't know the Christian lingo of what to say to describe it. I didn't know how to say that I was blessed by the Holy Spirit and felt His presence from head to toe. This kind of language was foreign to me and foreign to most outside the body of Christ. There is a world outside the four walls of our churches that doesn't walk or talk like us, and our Christianese is like another language to them.

When I got up, I sat on an altar that ran across the front of our church. I thought to myself, *I hope this feeling never goes away.* And I kept getting higher and higher in God's presence. Then I thought to myself, *I'm highly intoxicated, but in a new way—I don't feel dirty on the inside.* I felt clean and pure from head to toe. People were being hit by the power of God all over the room. A mist filled the room that night. I later came to realize that it was the shekinah glory of God. Then I said to myself, *If my friends who are hooked on drugs could feel this power that's going through me, they would follow Jesus.* At that moment I committed my life to the cause of Christ and the Gospel!

I walked into church that night bound with addiction and tormented by thoughts of death, hell, and the grave. I walked out saved, delivered, and filled with the fire of the Holy Spirit. As I walked out the doors of the church that night, I looked up to God and said, "My life for the Gospel!" I walked in bound by the devil, and walked out set free, called to be an evangelist. God is good! *When we weren't looking for God, He was looking for us.*

> When we weren't looking for
> God, He was looking for us.

The next Friday, I began attending the Brownsville Revival in Pensacola, Florida, which was about 90 minutes from where I lived. The evangelist whom God used to lead the revival was Steve Hill. He was a powerful evangelist with an anointing for repentance like no other I've ever been around in my life. He would preach on hell and holiness with the fire and conviction of the Holy Spirit. It would fill the room and was second to none. So my first vocabulary word as a baby Christian was *hell*.

After evangelist Steve Hill would give the altar call, wherein hundreds would respond every night for around five years, they would always pray for everyone hungry for more of God. This was a time when God moved in ways that would blow your mind every single night. Thousands would come from all over the world (even without social media we have today) and wait to be prayed for. Dr. Michael Brown was famous for praying *fire* over people. This comes from the passage in Luke 3:16 where John the Baptist said, *"One who is more powerful than I will come, the straps of whose sandals I am not worthy to untie. He will baptize you with the Holy Spirit and fire."* Often the power of God would hit people when he would pray. So my first two vocabulary words as a Christian were *hell* and *fire*.

I went to work the Friday prior to my salvation going to hell, and after I went back to work the following week I was telling everybody that they were going to go to hell if they didn't get right with God. Before I got saved, people liked me at work. But after I told them they were going to hell, I wasn't liked so much anymore. This wasn't the most effective form of evangelism, but I had to let what was on the inside of me come out, and my heart was to pull them out of hell even though I had never read Mathew 28 or Acts 1:8. No one sat me down and said this is what Christians are supposed to do; it just came natural as I could not contain what Jesus had done in my life.

Unfortunately, I couldn't find many people who were as fired up and eager to share the Gospel as I was. So often, I would do evangelism all by myself, which was honestly very dangerous. Remember, I wasn't saved long at all and my two vocabulary words were *hell* and *fire*. I would walk up to people in the mall and say, "Hello, my name is Joe Oden. If you died right now, would you go to heaven or hell?" One day not long after I was saved, I did this to a man in the mall. I asked him that question and looked at him with a very serious look in my eyes. My face was probably snarled up a bit because this was a serious matter. I had no idea how many people thought I seemed mad and a bit half-cocked. I was just trying my best to tell people of the goodness of God and what He had done in my life. People probably thought, *I've never met this guy in my life, and he just walks up to me and asks if I am going to heaven or hell. This guy is crazy.*

One particular day a gentleman responded, "I am a Baptist." I thought to myself, *There won't be one Assemblies of God, Baptist, Methodist, or Lutheran in heaven, just people washed in the blood of Jesus.* So I began to look for something to bust him on—one of those many things you could go to hell for that evangelist Steve Hill would preach about every night. I can't remember if it was cigarettes or chewing tobacco I saw in his pocket, but when I did I said, "You're not going to heaven but to hell for that tobacco." When I said that, he looked at me like I was crazy. For sure, he didn't feel the love of God and desire to come to my church and have me disciple him. He probably thought I was loco. He was right, but my heart was pure. I'm not sure why, but when I asked if I could pray for him, he let me! He probably thought I was going to go to church and pray with grandma for him in private. He had no idea I was about to lay hands on him publicly and pray the power of God down on his life. I probably yelled *fire* and completely tripped him out. Not only did I tell him he was going to hell, now I'm praying fire on him. There is no telling what was going through his head, but I bet it was, *Get me away from this guy!*

I wonder if Jesus was somewhere in heaven thinking, "Check this guy out!" And Gabriel and Michael likely responded, "Yes, we're checking him out, and he's out of control! Would You like us to stop him?" I'm sure Jesus encouraged them to stick things out because I hadn't read the Bible yet, and it would help me out a lot.

One night a guest minister was at my church and had a word for me, "You need to read the Bible." Wouldn't it be great if all evangelists read the Bible? So I began reading the Bible. I read Psalm 133 where it says that oil was poured on Aaron the priest from the top of his head to the bottom of his feet. I thought that sounded like a great idea, so I went and bought a big bottle of olive oil.

We prayed over the bottle of oil for about two weeks and then one night we uncorked it and I dumped it all over my friend's head. Then he did the same for me. It was around midnight, so where could we go to evangelize? Wal-Mart! It's open twenty-four hours a day, so that sounded like a great place to go. We walked in like we had been on a crystal methamphetamine binge. We had yellow stuff all over us and it had to be dripping on the floor. It looked like our "Depends" had broken wide open on aisle seven. It truly had to have been a sight to behold. One man walked up to us and said, "Excuse me, sir, but what is that in your hair? Have you been running?" I looked him straight in the eyes and let him know that we hadn't been running as he supposed, but we had anointed ourselves with oil and had come there to preach the Gospel. I'm confident he was tripped out. We probably laid hands on him and prayed down the fire of God. I'm sure he left that place wondering what in the world just happened to him.

> He wants people no matter their gifting or talent to simply be available. Are you available?

Now what was Jesus saying to Gabriel and Michael? Could he have been saying, "I like these dudes—they're available"?

People may be able to out-preach, out-teach, and out-sing you on talent or gift alone, but only you determine how available you are. Many may have better communication skills, or a more charismatic personality, and possess better social skills. However, that's not on the top of God's list for what He's looking for. He wants people no matter their gifting or talent to simply be available. Are you available?

If it were simply about talent and ability, then Jesus would not have needed to die and the Holy Spirit wouldn't have needed to come. The power is not in our talent and skill set; it's in the Gospel. Romans 1:16: *"For I am not ashamed of the gospel, because it is the power of God that brings salvation."* The power is in God's Word through your mouth. Second Corinthians 12:9 says, *"But he said to me, 'My grace is sufficient for you, for my power is made perfect in weakness.' Therefore I will boast all the more gladly about my weaknesses, so that Christ's power may rest on me."* In your weakness, Christ is made strong. So if you feel unequipped and weak to move in God's power, still His strength can and will move through your life.

I attended Bible school in Pensacola at the Brownsville Revival School of Ministry. I thrived in outreach and evangelism, and it had become my chief passion in life. From there, I left for the mission field. I had determined within myself to not just sit back and soak in God's presence at the revival, but I wanted to move out and share what I had. It was time to move out. My plan was that if I didn't receive a clear word from God, I would head for Thailand. So that's what I did. I had a good time preaching the Gospel and traveling the nation winning souls. From there I moved to Europe and traveled as an international evangelist for a season. Then, God spoke to me to move back to the United

States of America. When I was on the mission field, my burden was more for America than anywhere else.

America is not the great Gospel enterprise any longer and we need missions work here like never before. This is not the same nation of the greatest generation of World War II. Things have dramatically changed.

> America is not the great Gospel enterprise any longer and we need missions work here like never before.

Shortly after returning to America, I was sitting in a sandwich shop and ordered a nice chicken club. About that time, two girls walked in wearing provocative short-shorts. I thought to myself, "These girls need Jesus and are in danger of hell." I was going to tell them if they don't get right with God, they're headed to hell. But the Lord spoke to me and said, "You better not do that." I told God I was just letting Him know I'm *available.*

I then felt the Lord tell me that instead of condemning them, I could stand up and ask if there is anyone who is sick, addicted, or depressed. "Tell them you serve Me and that I will set them free right now if they will come and receive prayer." I agreed that His strategy was much better than mine. I chose not to correct them, and instead looked for an opportunity to make this proclamation.

Not long afterward, I was in a Mexican restaurant and felt God wanted me stand up and proclaim what He had given me. I was very nervous! However, I did not let fear paralyze me and I stood up and said, "Hello, my name is Joe Oden. If there is anyone here sick, addicted, or depressed, I would like to pray for you. I serve Jesus Christ and He will set you free if you let me pray for you."

When I sat down, this man from the other side of the room stood up and walked over to my table. He was weeping under the presence of God and he lifted up his hands to heaven and said, "I'm going through a divorce. Could you please pray for me and my kids who are sitting over there?" We laid hands on him and the power of God hit him right in the middle of the restaurant where everyone could see. The Holy Spirit filled the restaurant. I love it when that happens. Before he left, he told my friend that God had just changed his life. Second Timothy 1:7 says, *"For God has not given us a spirit of fear, but of power and of love and of a sound mind"* (NKJV). This day I chose to walk that scripture out beyond just agreeing with it. We must act upon what we agree with. We shouldn't have one without the other. I'd love to say I never let fear get the best of me, but I have at times. I choose not to focus on the moments I've let that happen, but on what could happen if I step out and am obedient in the future.

It's much easier to simply agree with the Word of God or an exciting line of a sermon. It doesn't take a whole lot to say "amen" out loud in a service or in your heart with no one even knowing. The world around us needs much more at this moment in history than believers simply *agreeing* with what God said. The time is at hand for *action*. If all believers took action on just half of what they agreed with, they would change the world. It's time for action in what we believe. This is what will change the world.

> *Thus also faith by itself, if it does not have works, is dead* (James 2:17 NKJV).

Dear Jesus, I ask You today to use me right where I am. Forgive me for the times I have felt Your nudge, but did not make myself available. Lord, help me overcome any fear of sharing You with others. I commit to being available for You to use me as You please. Jesus hear my confession today. I'm available; use me.

Chapter 2

TOUCHING HEAVEN, CHANGING EARTH

After coming to Christ, the prayer principle was alive on the inside of me. I hadn't been taught it beforehand. When God delivered me from drugs and alcohol through a supernatural encounter, I thought to myself, "If my friends only knew this powerful God and experienced His power firsthand, they would give their lives to Him." So I began to tenaciously go after God in prayer and fasting, pleading for the supernatural power of God to fall on me and release an anointing that would break bondages off of people bound and helpless. As I think back, it was so pure because my main prayer was that God would give me the power to see people slain in the Spirit. I prayed that way because that is what happened to me when I first experienced God in a tangible way. After I got off the floor from an encounter of a lifetime, I wanted everyone to have that same encounter. With that being said, it doesn't matter if you fall, shake, or just stand quietly, God can release His power however He wishes. This was just all I knew in my new experience and relationship with the Lord.

> After I got off the floor from an encounter of a lifetime, I wanted everyone to have that same encounter.

After praying for about three months that God would use me in this fashion, God used me this way in my home church one Sunday. I was praying for an elder in the church and he was hit by the power and fell to the ground. It was a powerful encounter for us both. As a young believer, I saw God answer my prayer to be used in a specific way to release the power of the Holy Spirit. I thought to myself, "God, if You can do this in a church, You can do this in the most wicked and vile places of the city!" So that's where I began to go.

I set out for downtown Mobile, Alabama, to a place that has similarities to the famous Bourbon Street in downtown New Orleans. The setting was a mixed bag of pimps, prostitutes, drug dealers, transvestites, a large number of gay bars, college-age partiers, alcoholics, and drug addicts. With the foundation of how God delivered me, I knew that there was *nothing* impossible for God.

I spent the majority of my Friday nights and often Saturday nights on the streets of downtown Mobile. I would pray and believe God would use me to see the captive set free. I would approach individuals who were bound and ask them a simple question, "Have you ever felt the power of God?" I had an answer for however they responded. If they answered, "No," I would simply ask, "Would you like to?" If they said, "Yes," I would simply ask, "Would you like to again?" After they would express that they were open to experiencing God's power, I would receive their permission to lay hands on them for prayer.

I can't tell you how many individuals I laid hands on before I finally witnessed an above-normal, powerful manifestation, outside of the local church. Many would say they had felt the power of God, but I was hungry for a visible, life-changing encounter to occur!

Through this process of praying and not seeing what I had been earnestly seeking, it caused me to press in more. I wasn't discouraged because I knew God would hear my cry. Oftentimes, I would go by myself, which I would not recommend, but this deepened my burden to see bondages broken. I remember one Friday night at around midnight just sitting up against an old rusted-out fence, in front of around five or six gay bars, praying and weeping for people to get free and experience God. I wasn't praying for a massive ministry, a platform, or finances. I just longed for an open heaven and for chains to be broken over Mobile. God was teaching me what it was to carry a burden and allowing me to feel His heart for people who didn't know Him.

It all starts at the place of prayer—everything that God wants to do through you. Why else does the devil discourage saints to cultivate an active prayer life? He fully understands the power of prayer, because anyone who has ever inflicted damage on his kingdom was a person of prayer. Moses, Daniel, Esther, Nehemiah, Jeremiah, Elijah, Elisha, David, John the Baptist, Peter, Paul, and our greatest example, Jesus Christ, just to name a few. They changed history through intercessory prayer!

Everything God has done and will do through us is birthed, maintained, and sustained in prayer. Jesus has given us many examples to encourage us to persevere in prayer:

> *Then Jesus told his disciples a parable to show them that they should always pray and not give up. He said: "In a certain town there was a judge who neither feared God nor cared what people thought. And there was a widow in that town who kept coming to him with the plea, 'Grant me justice against my adversary.' For some time he refused. But finally he said to himself, 'Even though I don't fear God or care what people think, yet because this widow keeps bothering me, I will see that she gets justice, so that she won't eventually come and attack me!'" And the Lord said, "Listen to what the unjust judge says. And will not God bring about justice for his chosen ones, who cry out to him day and night? Will he keep putting them off? I tell you, he will see that they get justice, and quickly"* (Luke 18:1-8).

God is looking for a praying man or a praying woman for a region or city, to put His burden upon them to pray until He opens heaven.

Jesus gave His disciples a great word, "Pray and never give up." It would've been easy for this widow to have thrown in the towel and walked away, especially if led by her emotions and the initial results. But instead of giving in she pressed in, even to the

point of intimidating the judge! She had a very powerful stance—
a made-up mind. There is tremendous power in a mind that is
made up. When we lay hold of spiritual truth and principles and
refuse to take "no" for an answer, no matter how long the wait,
victory is only a few steps away.

> ## You are the only person in
> ## your particular spot.

God is looking for a praying man or a praying woman for
a region or city, to put His burden upon them to pray until He
opens heaven. He's done it in the past; He'll do it again. Are you
that person? I said, *"Are you that person?"* This world is in desperate need for this ministry again, for individuals to have an
old-fashioned burden for people to be saved and God's Kingdom
to invade the particular spot God has placed them. *You are that
person, for you are the only person in your particular spot.*

This calling reminds me of the great prayer warrior
Nehemiah. He had a great burden for his people to be free as well:

> They said to me, "Those who survived the exile and
> are back in the province are in great trouble and dis-
> grace. The wall of Jerusalem is broken down, and
> its gates have been burned with fire." When I heard
> these things, I sat down and wept. For some days I
> mourned and fasted and prayed before the God of
> heaven (Nehemiah 1:3-4).

Nehemiah experienced a great burden for God to bring restoration to His people. Great destruction had taken place. This

is a good parallel to the culture today. Morality is broken down today, with gay marriage, abortion, the high rate of out of wedlock pregnancies, the legalization of drugs, godliness rejected in every corner of society. We need a burden like Nehemiah had.

He sat down and wept, fasted, and prayed. He was a layman in the king's palace. He wasn't a professional preacher or a prophet; he simply had a burden and wasn't going to enjoy the delicacies at his disposal. He was in mourning for a move of God. Ask yourself the question, "When was the last time I sat down and simply wept over a generation that is growing up in a society that promotes, relishes, and embraces a totally heathen society?" Barring a move of God, the next generation could pay the price for what we failed to pray.

We are in desperate need for praying men, women, families, and churches to simply ask God to use them in their day-to-day life, to release God's power and make a difference one conversation at a time. God heard Nehemiah's prayer and brought great deliverance and freedom. But it was birthed and forged through great anguish and prayer. God, let this burden fall on us again!

I consistently cried out for my city through fasting and prayer. Even though I wasn't seeing the manifestation of what was in my heart, I was determined not to give up and let go. Oftentimes people give up in prayer because of what they see or don't see. Discouragement sets in and they allow their emotions to override or build a false principle around what God is not doing or hasn't done.

I love what one of my spiritual heroes, evangelist Reinhard Bonnke, said once. He said that if he were asked what he would do if he prayed for 200 sick people and not one was healed, he would pray for the 201st like all 200 sick people were healed! He went on to say that he doesn't pray for the sick because of the results he gets, but because it's what God told us to do.

> *And these signs will accompany those who believe: In my name they will drive out demons; they will speak in new tongues; they will pick up snakes with their hands; and when they drink deadly poison, it will not hurt them at all; they will place their hands on sick people, and they will get well* (Mark 16:17-18; see also Luke 4:14-19; Acts 4:29-31).

Talk is cheap. How we respond to God through our **actions** reveals what we truly believe.

Talk is cheap. How we respond to God through our *actions* reveals what we truly believe. Are we willing to pray even if we don't see results? When we meditate on what God is not doing instead of what God has done or is doing, we literally sit down at the table the devil himself has prepared for us and partake of the great poison for the saints—doubt and unbelief. So when we pray we must heed the words of Christ, *"Always pray and never give up."*

After about a year and a half of developing a burden and continually praying for the bound in Mobile, unbeknownst to me I was on the verge of a major breakthrough. I was on the fourth or fifth day of a fast in downtown Mobile one Saturday night like countless times before. I asked a gay man if he had ever felt the power of God and he said he hadn't. I replied with my usual response, "Would you like to?" He said he would and gave me permission to lay hands on him and pray. When I prayed, just like every other time with faith and expectation as if everyone I had ever prayed for was hit by the power, a bolt of power fell like the lightning of God! This man was slain in the Spirit and fell down upon the concrete sidewalk without warning—no background music or someone to catch his fall—just the raw power of God. It was the power manifestation I had been longing for and that I knew with all my heart God could do. He got up after a moment and I led him to Christ. I didn't need to convince him that God was real—he had a firsthand encounter. It was actually very easy. He had tasted of the goodness of God. I love what Leonard Ravenhill once said and I believe this with all of my heart: *America doesn't need another definition of Christianity; she needs a demonstration of Christianity.* He went home that night having met Jesus through a demonstration of power.

Something changed in me that night. I stepped into a fresh, new anointing. No one could ever tell me God couldn't move in whatever way He chose and wherever He had a vessel to move through. After that night, I saw God move in this manner over and over and over again. A scripture that rings true to this on another level, but has similarities, is from King David:

> *Jesse had seven of his sons pass before Samuel, but Samuel said to him, "The Lord has not chosen these." So he asked Jesse, "Are these all the sons you have?" "There is still the youngest," Jesse answered. "He is tending the sheep." Samuel said, "Send for him; we will not sit down until he arrives." So he sent for him and had him brought in. He was glowing with health*

*and had a fine appearance and handsome features.
Then the Lord said, "Rise and anoint him; this is the
one." So Samuel took the horn of oil and anointed him
in the presence of his brothers, and from that day on
the Spirit of the Lord came powerfully upon David.
Samuel then went to Ramah* (1 Samuel 16:10-13).

Three powerful truths can be found in this passage:

1. Samuel instructed everyone, *"We will not sit
   down until he arrives."* He was communicating
   that we will not enjoy any more food and rest until the anointing has a place to rest. This should
   be our position before God. We will take no spiritual rest until we are walking and manifesting
   the anointing that God has for our life.

2. We are going to show God honor by placing a high honor on the anointing. The anointing is precious and has no monetary price tag.
   Therefore, we must reverently position ourselves
   in God's sight, eagerly praying and waiting for
   the fullness God has intended for us.

3. After the anointing oil fell upon David, *"From
   that day on, the Spirit of the Lord came powerfully upon David."* This tells us that God desires
   His power and anointing to rest upon us continu-
   ously and undiminished. From that day on it never departed from David. God grant every reader
   this amazing gift that will never depart, in the
   name of Jesus.

We must reverently position ourselves in God's sight, eagerly praying and waiting for the fullness God has intended for us.

Walking in Prayer

Ask and it will be given to you; seek and you will find; knock and the door will be opened to you. For everyone who asks receives; the one who seeks finds; and to the one who knocks, the door will be opened. Which of you, if your son asks for bread, will give him a stone? Or if he asks for a fish, will give him a snake? If you, then, though you are evil, know how to give good gifts to your children, how much more will your Father in heaven give good gifts to those who ask him! (Matthew 7:7-11)

We see a clear process God gives us to receive answered prayer. He gives us three distinct approaches and repeats Himself. So this is without a doubt a picture of walking in prayer. This can and has been demonstrated over and over to receive a fresh anointing throughout the Word of God (see Acts 2).

Christ repeats Himself to make His point clear. He first instructs us to *ask*. There are many things in life that you have to ask for if you want to receive them. If you are in a particular restaurant, you don't expect the waiter or waitress to know what you want them to bring you; you ask. After you ask, they will grant your request. How much more loving is God to grant us our request, especially if it's the request for a fresh empowerment to see the lost come to Him and move in the power of His Spirit?

> *Which of you, if your son asks for bread, will give him a stone? Or if he asks for a fish, will give him a snake? If you, then, though you are evil, know how to give good gifts to your children, how much more will your Father in heaven give good gifts to those who ask him!*

We see another clear example of this with Bartimaeus.

> *Jesus stopped and ordered the man to be brought to him. When he came near, Jesus asked him, "What do you want me to do for you?" "Lord, I want to see," he replied. Jesus said to him, "Receive your sight; your faith has healed you." Immediately he received his sight and followed Jesus, praising God. When all the people saw it, they also praised God* (Luke 18:40-43; see also Mark 10:46-52).

Jesus fully understood what he needed, but He wanted to hear it from him. Just as you are specific with many requests to God, be specific and ask God for a fresh anointing to impact the world around you.

Knock and the door will be opened is another powerful key. If a neighbor's house were to catch on fire in the middle of the night and they were unaware, I would not just go and give a gentle knock at the door and if no one answered just assume they did not want to be disturbed. I would beat on the door and get an axe if need be; I would not stop until they knew I was there and I received a response. This is the way God wants us to seek Him.

He wants us to knock until the door is opened. He promised the door would open; we just have to knock until it is.

Seek and you will find. I don't know about you, but I have been known to lose my keys from time to time. It always seems to happen when I have an important meeting that I have to attend. I'll search the house over, turning upside down the couch cushions, going through every room and every possible place they could be. Why? Because I'm not leaving until they are found. Some seek their keys or a lost possession with more intensity than they do walking in a fresh anointing. If we seek God for a fresh anointing, He will answer us and we will find that anointing. We just have to pursue by asking, seeking, and knocking.

> If we seek God for a fresh anointing, He will answer us and we will find that anointing. We just have to pursue by asking, seeking, and knocking.

The woman with the unjust judge did not give up until she was granted justice—from a judge who didn't fear God or care about people, but because of her persistence, her petition was granted. Her mind was made up that she was not going to quit until she had justice.

Let's make up our minds, like Samuel, and not sit down until the anointing has a place to rest. As the blind man Jesus healed cried, "Jesus, son of David, have mercy on me." He would not be denied until he was healed. As Nehemiah fasted and prayed until the city was rebuilt and victory was at hand. Let us now bow before God before reading any more, for God to pour out His anointing and Holy Spirit upon us in a fresh way to empower us to destroy the works of hell and use us in dimensions we have not yet walked. Ask God to give you tenacious faith as Jacob had as he told God, "I will not let you go until you bless me."

God, we have made up our minds—we will not let You go until we are walking in the fullness of Your supernatural power to impact a lost and hurting world like never before! I pray for a deep burden for the lost. Let me have Your mind and Your heart toward every person around me who does not know You. Please put a divine frustration in me that is moved to fast and pray until I am walking in the fullness of Your power and anointing that You have called me to walk in. In Jesus's name. Amen.

Chapter 3

FAITH: CONNECTING WITH GOD'S POWER

One evening I was in a famous bookstore and felt led to enter one of the select sections for someone who would be in need of Jesus—the witchcraft section. To the natural man, this may not look like the best place to meet someone ripe and ready to be approached with the message of Christ.

As I waited in this particular section for several moments, I was hoping and praying that someone bound by the devil would come look at the books in that area. Then, a young man walked up and started looking through the books. I was very excited to see the next candidate about to experience the delivering power of God. When I approached him, I asked him a question, "Is there any power in these books?" He replied immediately, "Oh yeah!" He went on to tell me about this long, drawn-out encounter he had with a demon manifesting in his room. He told me how the demon was opening and shutting drawers without anyone touching them. He went on to tell me how one fell out and hit the ground and screws went everywhere. This man was a firm believer in the powers of hell.

When he finished telling me his story, I told him, "There is a lot more power in the name of Jesus and the Holy Spirit than every devil." Needless to say, he didn't like my response. He became angry and went off on me for about ten minutes. I wouldn't have been surprised if he physically attacked me. I just listened and didn't argue with him. I've never argued anyone into the Kingdom of God or into having an encounter with the power of the Holy Spirit. It is a good rule of thumb whenever you are engaged with an unbeliever to listen to them fully no matter how outlandish their statements may be. It's just rude to interrupt them, and I knew he was quite upset.

When he finished speaking, I just asked him a simple question: "Have you ever felt the power of God?" He said, "No." I said, "Would you like to?" He said, "Yes." Wow! Everything changed in the flash of a moment. I asked for permission to lay hands upon him, and as I did I began to pray a very simple prayer, "Lord, I ask You tonight, when this man gets back to his truck, that You would touch him with Your fire." He looked at me and said, "How did you know I have a truck?" I said, "I didn't." This was a subtle word of knowledge that slipped out in prayer, which is one of the nine gifts of the Spirit. His whole demeanor and countenance changed. He wasn't angry anymore and it was completely obvious that God had touched him. At that moment we both went our separate ways.

About one year later I was with a friend of mine and we were about to do an outreach in a bar district. She informed me that a few months earlier while in a church service a man stood up and said, "I've got to tell everyone how I got saved. I was in the bookstore in the witchcraft section and this guy came over to me and got me to engage with him about the demonic realm. Then he brought up Jesus. I was so angry I was about to punch him in the face. But then he asked if he could pray for me, and for some reason I let him. As he prayed, he mentioned God touching me when I get back to my truck. I knew he couldn't have known I had a truck. He went on to pray that the fire of God would touch me. When he left, within five minutes, all I can say is that what he prayed manifested—the fire of God fell on me right then and there. I got on my knees and gave my life to Jesus Christ and have been living for God ever since. That night completely changed my life."

> His whole demeanor and countenance changed. He wasn't angry anymore and it was completely obvious that God had touched him.

With that being said, had I fixed my eyes on the bondage that I could see rather than the God I could not see, I would have missed God completely. We must never be intimidated by the bondage, sickness, false religion, addictions, or strongholds that we can see. We must fix our eyes on the God we cannot see because He has the power to break every bondage that we can see.

One of the major obstacles for many Christians who are sold out to Christ oftentimes isn't their dedication or their pursuit of God; it's their applying God's Word to pierce the kingdom of darkness. It's not that many don't agree with God's Word—it's putting it in action to change the world around us. For instance, it's easy to "Amen" a power scripture like *"The one who is in you is greater than the one who is in the world"* (1 John 4:4). But to live our lives in sync with this power is another story.

When we come in contact with individuals who are bound by the spirit of this age, we will often put more faith in the bondage that we see, rather than Christ in us whom we can't see. Ask yourself this question: When I see someone addicted or bound by a false religion, do my actions manifest the power of Christ in me, causing me to take action and engage those in bondage to see the strongholds broken?

Here is a very powerful scripture that is key to moving in the power of God and taking control of what we can see:

> *So we fix our eyes not on what is seen, but on what is unseen, since what is seen is temporary, but what is unseen is eternal* (2 Corinthians 4:18).

If you are not ministering to individuals because of the work of darkness in their life, your eyes are fixed on what you can see rather than on what you can't see. It's not enough to agree by faith with a scripture or a talking point—we must live it out.

> *In the same way, faith by itself, if it is not accompanied by action, is dead. But someone will say, "You have faith; I have deeds." Show me your faith without deeds, and I will show you my faith by my deeds. You believe that there is one God. Good! Even the demons believe that—and shudder. You foolish person, do you want evidence that faith without*

deeds is useless? Was not our father Abraham considered righteous for what he did when he offered his son Isaac on the altar? You see that his faith and his actions were working together, and his faith was made complete by what he did. And the scripture was fulfilled that says, "Abraham believed God, and it was credited to him as righteousness," and he was called God's friend. You see that a person is considered righteous by what they do and not by faith alone. In the same way, was not even Rahab the prostitute considered righteous for what she did when she gave lodging to the spies and sent them off in a different direction? As the body without the spirit is dead, so faith without deeds is dead (James 2:17-26).

If the church took action on half the things we amen, we would shake the world.

When we say we believe in the power of God and that "Nothing is impossible for God!" our actions must show it. It's easy to shout *"amen!"* to a preacher at a point we agree with, but how do we handle it when we have to walk it out with someone who is bound? It's more than agreeing with "Greater is He that is in me than he that is in the world." If we really believed it, it should change us! We must walk it out and demonstrate it to a world that's suffering without Christ. If the church took action on half the things we amen, we would shake the world.

We would never *say* we have more faith in the works of darkness such as witchcraft, atheism, Islam, or homosexuality, but when we never lift a finger or a voice to see them set free outside the local church, our actions say we put more faith in the bondage we can see rather than the God we cannot see.

I love what the apostle Paul said: *"So we fix our eyes not on what is seen, but on what is unseen, since what is seen is temporary"* (2 Cor. 4:18). This is a spiritual discipline; if we so fix our eyes on the unseen, we will walk in the Spirit, actively putting our faith into action and stepping out and believing God to move through us to oppose the forces of darkness. Do this and watch the chains fall off prisoners, watch the dominion of Satan lose its captives!

The Greek word for *fix* in this particular passage is *skopeo*. The exact meaning of this word for this passage is "to watch out for, to take notice of, look to, fix eyes on, see to it, watch." So Paul is telling us not to look to, see to, take notice, fix eyes on, or watch what we can see, because it is temporary. So our stance, faith, and action should be in direct opposition to every stronghold and bondage that we can see, for it is temporary. This is great news!

This means that every addiction, false religion, sickness, all immorality, and everything that relates to the work of darkness has an expiration date on the back of it! So we should not give it a second glance. But the Kingdom of our God and the precious blood of Jesus Christ will last for all of eternity, and it has no expiration date. So we should *fix* our eyes on what is "unseen," for it is "eternal." Therefore, we should *skopeo*—watch out for, take notice of, look to, fix our eyes on—the God we cannot see, for He is eternal. The God we cannot "see" has the power and resources to break any and every bondage we can see. *Amen!* So let us not just agree, but take action with this powerful truth and invade the kingdom of darkness by faith.

Faith for Today

Many followers of Christ fit one of the three categories we will look at in this section. Our key text comes from John 11:

> *On his arrival, Jesus found that Lazarus had already been in the tomb for four days. Now Bethany was less than two miles from Jerusalem, and many Jews had come to Martha and Mary to comfort them in the loss of their brother. When Martha heard that Jesus was coming, she went out to meet him, but Mary stayed at home. "Lord," Martha said to Jesus, "if you had been here, my brother would not have died. But I know that even now God will give you whatever you ask." Jesus said to her, "Your brother will rise again." Martha answered, "I know he will rise again in the resurrection at the last day"* (John 11:17-24).

Martha was in a state of grieving for her brother who had recently passed away. She made a statement of faith for what God could have done at an earlier time: "*if you had been here, my brother would not have died.*" What Martha was saying is, "I have faith for what You could've done yesterday." That's where many in the body of Christ have placed their faith.

They have no problem believing that God performed miracles in the past or in days gone by. If you stood in a church and said that miracles never really happened, you would have a divided church on your hands. Many would talk about what God has done in the past, such as divine miracles, powerful healings, and deliverances. Many would argue with great conviction on "yesterday's" faith. Martha was basically saying, "Jesus I know You could have performed a miracle yesterday, a few days ago, but I don't have the faith to believe for today."

Then Jesus, moved with compassion, speaks life to her and tries to provoke her to believe: *"Your brother will rise again."* He was telling her not to fear, but believe! We see by her response that she didn't believe what He was saying. She said, *"I know he will rise again in the resurrection at the last day."* This statement represents a whole other sect of the body of Christ. She had great faith for tomorrow. She didn't doubt at all that it would happen; it would just be in the future.

That's where many are today. They believe for revival, which we all should, but it's somewhere out in the distance. That someday miracles will return, the heavens will open wider if we just pray and hold out long enough. I believe for this just as much as anyone. But the Word of God gives us a more encouraging word for the here and now, not just for what God did or one day will do.

> *Jesus, once more deeply moved, came to the tomb. It was a cave with a stone laid across the entrance. "Take away the stone," he said. "But, Lord," said Martha, the sister of the dead man, "by this time there is a bad odor, for he has been there four days." Then Jesus said, "Did I not tell you that if you believe, you will see the glory of God?" So they took away the stone. Then Jesus looked up and said, "Father, I thank you that you have heard me. I knew that you always*

hear me, but I said this for the benefit of the people standing here, that they may believe that you sent me." When he had said this, Jesus called in a loud voice, "Lazarus, come out!" The dead man came out, his hands and feet wrapped with strips of linen, and a cloth around his face. Jesus said to them, "Take off the grave clothes and let him go" (John 11:38-44).

Standing opposed to Lazarus's tomb, Jesus was going to demonstrate one of the most powerful truths in the Bible—that miraculous powers are not restricted by time. He will continue moving supernaturally today, tomorrow, and forevermore. He is the God of today, not just yesterday and tomorrow. With that one word of faith, *"Lazarus, come out!"* the dead man came out. Jesus showed humanity that He is the God of today!

> He will continue moving supernaturally today, tomorrow, and forevermore. He is the God of today!

The Bible makes it crystal clear: *"Jesus Christ is the same yesterday and today and forever"* (Heb. 13:8). So we not only believe in what God did yesterday or what God will do tomorrow, we *believe* that God can and will intervene on our behalf today. The same God who healed cancer yesterday heals cancer today. The same power of Christ that will raise the dead in the future is the same Christ who will raise the dead today. The same Jesus who walked on the water thousands of years ago to rescue the disciples is the same God who can walk right into the midst of your situation and rescue you *today. "I the Lord do not change"* (Mal. 3:6).

Let us apply this to our lives and ministry as we minister to people who need healing, salvation, and breakthroughs. We should carry this faith despite what we see, feel, or sense. Whatever the situation may be, let us apply this powerful truth and walk it out to tear down darkness and release God's Kingdom on earth as it is in heaven.

Walking It Out in a Practical Way

During a time on the mission field in the nation of England, I was about to go to bed from a long day of ministry. As I was finishing up a time of prayer, I felt impressed to pull out my day-timer and draw what God desired of me. Now this was *way* out of the box for me. I had never heard of this and I am a terrible artist. But I couldn't shake the impression, so I drew a simple drawing as I felt led. It was very simple. It was a stick man that was depressed with clouds hanging over its head. Then in another frame on the same page, two hands were coming out of the clouds representing the hands of God that had touched the depressed individual. Then I drew another stickman that was liberated and happy after God had touched its life. Immediately the burden left and I went to bed fulfilling what God wanted me to do.

The next day when we arrived at the church we were working with, I was told about a worship service for a CD release we were going to have at the church that night. As a part of the worship, they were going to have prophetic painting and art during the service. I thought that was incredibly cool because I had just felt led to draw the night before and had never heard of this within a church or worship service. I thought, "Man, I guess I'm in the flow!"

Later that morning, I walked across the street from the church into a mall and sat down at a coffee shop to have a latte. I was with a friend and as we were talking over coffee I looked up and saw what appeared to be a full-blown witch. She was dressed in solid black, white face paint covered her entire face, and rings were all over her face. The Lord spoke to me and said, "Go tell her that she believes in Jesus." That's all He said for me to do. Now I was told that England is less than five percent Christian, so not a lot of people believe. But I felt this was definitely a word of knowledge. I jumped up without time to spare and hurried after her and gave her the small word God had given me. She said, "I do believe in Jesus." Keep in mind, this did not line up at all with what I could physically see. She was nice and as we talked, she said she enjoyed painting. I told her we were having a worship service and they would be painting during that time. She said she would like to come and paint, so I felt this was awesome. God could definitely touch her tonight and it seemed to be a divine appointment.

She was dressed in solid black, white face paint covered her entire face, and rings were all over her face. The Lord spoke to me and said, "Go tell her that she believes in Jesus."

As the worship service started, I was on one side of the building worshiping and she was on the other side painting. About an hour into the service, I was curious to see what she was painting.

As I looked at what she painted, it was the same exact details from what I drew the night before! She had a person that was depressed on one side, then the hand of God coming down. Then she had another person who had been liberated by the touch of God who was now happy. I was amazed! I went and got my day-timer and showed her what I had drawn the night before. I then said, "Emma, last night I drew your salvation and tonight you drew yours, as well. God is speaking to you and wants you to give your life fully to Him." She did right then and there! It was glorious!

The next day we were going to do an outreach in the area. Emma showed up bright and early to go with the team and reach out to people who needed Christ. To my surprise, without anyone saying a word, Emma showed up with a completely different appearance. I didn't have anything against the way she was dressed, but apparently God gently dealt with her to lose the witch look.

After the day was coming to a close, she asked if she should still listen to Marilyn Manson. He is a very demonic singer/performer, from what I've read about him. Instead of telling her not to listen to it, I just suggested that she go home and pray about it. I could tell her, but I thought this would be a good time for her to hear God's voice for herself.

The next day she showed up to go on another outreach. I asked her if she had prayed and what she felt God tell her concerning Manson. She said she had several rock-n-roll groups all over her walls. Around 20 of her posters were Manson ones. When she woke up the next morning after praying about it the night before, all of the Manson posters were face down on the ground. None of the others were down. I knew God was already supernaturally speaking to her and told her so. This was a powerful move of the Spirit in this young lady's life. Ripping her from the kingdom of darkness and placing her into the Kingdom of Light!

God, I ask You to ground our faith—not in what we see but in what we cannot see. Lord, help us to fix our eyes on You and Your ability and not the bondage and captivity we see. Strengthen our faith in the things we cannot see rather than the works of hell we do see. "Now faith is confidence in what we hope for and assurance about what we do not see" (Heb. 11:1). Help us walk in complete trust that You truly are the same yesterday, today, and forever! God, as a believer-disciple trusting in Your grace, I commit to live out the truth You proved —You are the God of today and every day.

Chapter 4

WHEN ATMOSPHERES SHIFT

was privileged to attend the Brownsville Revival School of Ministry. This was an awesome time in my life. I had the opportunity to be a part of the longest-standing local church revival in the history of America. During my time in school, I was burdened for downtown Mobile. After God saw that I was faithful to pray, fast, and believe for my city, He added to our number. I would usually go by myself or with one or two others. Now God had given me a team from the Brownsville Revival School of Ministry.

What I started alone eventually grew to around 75 people at times. I tried to keep the team around 20–30 people. Our strategy was to lift up Christ through worship. We would have djembes, guitars, saxophones, and all kinds of small acoustic instruments. There were 20–30 bars in direct vicinity of our worship. It ranged over a four- to five-block area. We would literally march around and around the blocks singing and worshiping with all our heart, mind, and strength. We didn't care what anybody thought. We wanted heaven to invade earth. We understood that humanity was not our opposition, but the kingdom of darkness was. We believed the Word and joined the likes of Paul: *"For our struggle is not against flesh and blood, but against the rulers, against the authorities, against the powers of this dark world and against the spiritual forces of evil in the heavenly realms"* (Eph. 6:12).

Instead of focusing on what the enemy was doing, we focused on what God could do, and we desired to lift Him up so He would be invited into the atmosphere. It was a wild scene. A group of on-fire Christians marching through a drug-infested party atmosphere. Every weekend we would do this. The team would fast, pray, and believe by faith for a breakthrough.

Most nights we would end up at the corner of Conception and Conti street. This was the same area where the man was hit by the power and fell to the ground in Chapter Two. It seemed as if God wanted to shift the atmosphere on that corner with gay bars on practically every side of us.

One night the power of God seemed to be moving in a very powerful way. We were singing a very simple chorus: "Jesus, I adore You." I would tell the team not to focus initially on talking to people, but to focus on lifting up Christ and that He would set the atmosphere and do the drawing. Once the atmosphere was set, a few people would then begin talking with people surrounding us.

On this night, as we were totally focused on drawing near to God and Him drawing near to us, this guy heard us and wanted to put a stop to all the worship. He didn't like what we were doing.

No one was looking at him or engaged in a conversation with him; he was just sick of us being there at 11:00 PM. He decided to come hit one of my friends, blindside. He suddenly walked across the street and was ready to punch.

As he crossed the street to punch him, he stepped up on the corner where we were. Suddenly, with no one praying for him or saying a word to him, he was hit by the power of God and began to weep. In lightning speed, everything changed. He didn't pull his fist up to strike my friend but instead cried like a baby.

Winning people to Christ is much easier after they are touched by His power.

We led him to Christ right there on the spot. We didn't have to convince him that God was real. He just had a life-changing encounter with the Holy Ghost. *Winning people to Christ is much easier after they are touched by His power.* After we led him to Christ, we laid hands on him to pray. He got hit by the power of God and fell right into the street. No catch team or prep on how to receive from God. God just popped him right there and he fell right in the street.

After a moment or two, he got up off of the street still weeping and deeply moved by the Spirit of God. He began to tell us how he was a Vietnam veteran who had a deep-rooted seed of anger and violence. He then pulled a knife out of his pocket and handed it to my friend. He told us how he used to hurt people violently. He gave us the knife and said he no longer wanted to do that and that Jesus had set him free from a spirit of murder, anger, and violence. There had been a sea change in the atmosphere.

To be effective in shifting an atmosphere, especially out-side the four walls of the church, we need to apply what we have already looked at—prayer, fasting, and faith. With these three being the foundation, a powerful element to throw into the mix is worship. I've always been baffled at why anointed worship leaders don't often take their gifts to parking lots, parks, and bar districts to release God's presence.

Whenever I've led outreaches, whether it be one visit or for years at a time in the same location, I like to set up worship. I love the scripture, *"And I, when I am lifted up from the earth, will draw all people to myself"* (John 12:32). I take this verse literally. If we lift up Christ through praise and worship and glorify Him, He will draw men unto Himself. So this is exactly what we practice. This is exactly what drew the Vietnam vet.

The Lord's Prayer

This, then, is how you should pray; "Our Father in heaven, hallowed be your name, your kingdom come, your will be done, on earth as it is in heaven. Give us today our daily bread. And forgive us our debts, as we also have forgiven our debtors. And lead us not into temptation, but deliver us from the evil one" (Matthew 6:9-13).

That night two kingdoms collided. The kingdom of dark-ness (which manifested murder, anger, and violence) and the Kingdom of God. In this particular case, it was love, joy, peace, and mercy. When God's Kingdom and the devils' kingdom col-lide, the enemy has to bow and the Kingdom of God will reign. We brought heaven to earth that night. There is no murder, anger, or violence in heaven—just love, joy, peace, and mercy. So the kingdom of hell had to bow as the Kingdom of God ruled.

The Lord is looking for His ambassadors to release His Kingdom and decree. It doesn't matter if we feel like we are ambassadors; we are. We were set up on that corner as ambassadors. We understood who we were in Christ: "*We are therefore Christ's ambassadors, as though God were making his appeal through us. We implore you on Christ's behalf: Be reconciled to God*" (2 Cor. 5:20).

> The Lord is looking for His ambassadors to release His Kingdom and decree. It doesn't matter if we feel like we are ambassadors; we are.

The *Merriam-Webster* definition of *ambassador* reads, "The highest-ranking person who represents his or her own government while living in another country; appointed for a special and often temporary diplomatic assignment; an authorized representative or messenger." This is a powerful truth that we must attain if we are going to walk in fullness of God's authority and power here on earth.

Oftentimes we will read powerful accounts of God's chosen servants of years gone by—such as Moses, Esther, Gideon, Daniel, Jeremiah, Paul, Hannah, and Peter—and we will say, "I could never be used to operate as they were."

Let's take Moses for example. God moved mightily through him as His ambassador on earth. He was God's choice representative releasing God's decree and standing on His authority and word, not his own. As God directed, Moses witnessed miracle after miracle. Some of the things God did through his life, just to name a few, were the 10 plagues, the splitting of the Red Sea, following the cloud by day and the fire by night, manna from heaven, the quail, the healing miracles, and the mountain shaking. If we're honest, we've all looked at this at some point and thought, "I could never do that."

Another instance is Peter preaching the first Gospel message where people could be saved after the death of Christ and seeing 3,000 come to Christ. Remember, the ones who killed Jesus were in the crowd. This was a fearlessly bold act where he put his life on the line, proclaiming, *"Therefore let all Israel be assured of this: God has made this Jesus, whom you crucified, both Lord and Messiah"* (Acts 2:36).

Shortly afterward, God also used him in the healing of a crippled person:

> *Now a man who was lame from birth was being carried to the temple gate called Beautiful, where he was put every day to beg from those going into the temple courts. When he saw Peter and John about to enter, he asked them for money. Peter looked straight at him, as did John. Then Peter said, "Look at us!" So the man gave them his attention, expecting to get something from them. Then Peter said, "Silver or gold I do not have, but what I do have I give you. In the name of Jesus Christ of Nazareth, walk." Taking him by the right hand, he helped him up, and instantly the man's feet and ankles became strong. He jumped to his feet and began to walk. Then he went with*

them into the temple courts, walking and jumping, and praising God (Acts 3:2-8).

This was a notable miracle.

Remember Esther's raw faith in the face of possible death. *"Go, gather together all the Jews who are in Susa, and fast for me. Do not eat or drink for three days, night or day. I and my atten-dants will fast as you do. When this is done, I will go to the king, even though it is against the law. And if I perish, I perish"* (Esther 4:16). This was powerful faith and dedication to God in the face of death. Through this act of faith and prayer, her life was spared and the decree to eradicate the Jews was thwarted. Esther's brav-ery was breathtaking.

We will compare our weakness to their strength and often come to a conclusion that God could use them in extraordinary power, but not us. We see and glorify their faith at the pinna-cle and not as they were in the process. What was Moses's state of mind when God first called him? How about Peter? How did he respond to adverse circumstances during Christ's crucifixion (see Matt. 26:69–75), during a time when He needed his support more than ever? What was Esther's response to her uncle when she was made aware of the death sentence of her entire race (see Esther 4:1–14)?

Let's take a look in detail at how Moses responded to God as he was starting out. What did Moses's conversation with God after he was commissioned look like? Ask yourself if you've ever asked or made some of the statements of the great prophet Moses.

Here was his first question to God, *"Who am I that I should go to Pharaoh and bring the Israelites out of Egypt?"* (Exod. 3:11). Moses was afraid and did not feel he had the confidence to communicate before Pharaoh. He did not feel adequate to fulfill what God was asking him to do. Have you ever felt like that?

The reality is that Moses could not do it. He proved that fact forty years earlier when he killed a particular taskmaster who was beating his fellow Hebrew. He could not do it alone, that is: *"With man this is impossible, but with God all things are possible"* (Matt. 19:26). He tried to do it by himself at one time but learned a valuable lesson: apart from God you can do nothing. However, when we team up with God, we make an unbeatable team. God could do it by Himself but chose to use Moses. God assured Moses that He was with him wherever he went.

> *Moses said to God, "Suppose I go to the Israelites and say to them, 'The God of your fathers has sent me to you,' and they ask me, 'What is his name?' Then what shall I tell them?"* (Exodus 3:13)

This question, *"What is His name?"* can stand for any question you don't have the answer for. Moses was not sure what he should say. Have you ever thought, "I know God is calling me, but I don't know what to say or the answers to the questions I may be asked?" Maybe an honest concern you would have is, "I do not know the Bible well enough." Moses basically said the same thing. God knows our limitations and wants us to rely on His anointing and ability. It is okay to talk to God in order to receive understanding, and God is gracious to help.

God answered Moses in Exodus 3:14–22. He even gave him great prophetic insight about what would happen and how he would be received. He told Moses what to say to the people and to Pharaoh. Sometimes God will not give us the entire outline of His plan prior to us taking the first step. He may give us the first part and, when that is fulfilled, give us the second part.

Moses was doing a good thing in asking the Lord questions. The last time he stepped out, he did not first inquire of the Lord, and he paid a severe price for that crucial mistake. One of the greatest decisions David made before going out to fight was inquiring of the Lord about whether or not he should even go. God told him what to do. Joshua practiced the same principle. *This should be our constant prayer—talking to the Lord about how to react in a situation that God has called us to.* When God responds to us after we pray, it is called an "answered prayer." That is the right way to approach anything God calls us to do. Talk to Him thoroughly about it; get His perspective and trust Him through it all—no matter the cost.

> This should be our constant prayer— talking to the Lord about how to react in a situation that God has called us to.

Moses had yet another question, *"What if they do not believe me or listen to me and say, 'The Lord did not appear to you'?"* (Exod. 4:1). Have you ever thought to yourself, "What if they do not listen to me or believe what I am telling them is the truth?" Wow! If you answered *yes*, you are more like Moses than you think.

The Bible is true when it says, *"Jesus Christ is the same yesterday and today and forever"* (Heb. 13:8). If God gave a sign to the people Moses was sent to, He can do the same for us today. We must believe, however, that God will move on our behalf when we go out in faith and obedience.

God's response to Moses was powerful. He basically told him of several miracles He would perform through him (see Exod. 4:1–9). In First Corinthians 12, this type of display of power would fall under the gift of miracles. This power is available to us through the baptism of the Holy Spirit, which we will look at in more depth later. Again, God let Moses know exactly what to do. God will also do the same for us today.

The story of Moses also addresses another concern believers have about witnessing: *"Moses said to the Lord, 'Pardon your servant, Lord. I have never been eloquent, neither in the past nor since you have spoken to your servant. I am slow of speech and tongue'"* (Exod. 4:10). Moses made a statement that most of the body of Christ makes quite frequently. Moses was focusing on his own abilities and strengths. He was looking at what he could do and not what God could do. Many times, we will step out and do what God says only as long as we can do it in our own ability and strength. That's not ministering in the fire power of God— that's ministering in our own feeble power!

> We must take our eyes off what we can make happen and look to God for what He can make happen through us.

We must take our eyes off what we can make happen and look to God for what He can make happen through us. When the world sees the church moving in something they cannot produce, buy, or make happen, they will come and fill the house of

God throughout the world. God wanted Moses to look at what He could do through him and not what Moses could do by himself. When we begin to have this mindset in our day-to-day life, we will see atmospheres shift and God's Kingdom advance.

He still lacked confidence. He had little trust in God. Even though God was giving him the power to fulfill the mission, he still did not want to go. Many who are saved and filled with the Spirit still say, "I can't." There isn't much more you need than God dwelling in you. Many Christians still don't step out radically because they really don't know or trust in what God can and will do through them; they only trust in their own abilities. This is the very mindset that God was trying to break off of Moses. It is the very thing He longs to break off the body of Christ. The church *can* go forward in power.

Now the Lord began to question Moses: "*Who gave human beings their mouths? Who makes them deaf or mute? Who gives them sight or makes them blind? Is it not I, the Lord? Now go; I will help you speak and will teach you what to say*" (Exod. 4:11-12). The Lord wanted Moses to understand that His ability more than made up for the inability of man. God said to him: "Am I not the one who made you? I am bigger than your perceived personal limitations. I made you, and I can fix anything that needs to be fixed. I understand human anatomy, and I understand you, Moses. You can do this because I have chosen you. Do not trust in *your* ability, but *Mine*." God was communicating to him, "When I called you, I was fully aware of your speaking ability." God wanted him to know, "It's not about how well you can or can't speak. It's not about your charisma or your social skills. It's about *Me* moving in and through you, and that's more than enough."

But Moses said, "Pardon your servant, Lord. Please send someone else." Then the Lord's anger burned against Moses and he said, "What about your brother, Aaron the Levite? I know he can speak well. He is already on his way to meet you, and he will be glad to see you. You shall speak to him and put words in his mouth; I will help both of you speak and will teach you what to do. He will speak to the people for you, and it will be as if he were your mouth and as if you were God to him. But take this staff in your hand so you can perform the signs with it" (Exodus 4:13-17).

Moses said to the Lord, "O Lord, please send someone else to do it." Have you ever asked God to allow someone else to fulfill what He has asked you to do? That was the one statement God did not like at all. He understood all of the other things Moses said, but when he told the Lord to send someone else, God was not happy. *"Then the Lord's anger burned against Moses."* This made the Lord very angry. It makes God angry when we want Him to get someone else do what He has called *us* to accomplish. This is one clear way to make God angry—ask Him to send someone else to do what He has called you to do.

> This is one clear way to make God angry—ask Him to send someone else to do what He has called you to do.

We might not use the words of Moses, but we often say the same things. For example, you may pray for God to save someone, but if you never share the Gospel with them, you are asking God to do the job He gave you to do, ignoring our Lord's last commandment to go into all the world and make disciples (see Matt. 28:19-20). The book of Jude says to snatch others from the fire and *save* them (see Jude 23). God has called us to *save* and be a *light*. We ask God to stop abortion but have never been the voice of salvation for babies at a clinic. Many ask God to heal, but never lay hands on the sick. We must absolutely ask God for these things, but then we must act on our prayer, being doers of the Word and not hearers only.

If you have been guilty of this in the past, do not fall under condemnation; just repent and ask God to forgive you. Then begin to walk in what He has called you to do. If it is evangelism, tell someone about Jesus before the day is out! Whatever it may be, just do it and watch God move.

God was basically saying: "When you go, I will show." Moses going out was God coming down. God will not just pop out of heaven; we must go. Our going out is God coming down. He always chooses to use people. The rest is history—Moses went out and God came down. The atmosphere in Egypt didn't shift due to a prayer meeting alone. The Hebrews weren't set free until Moses showed up in person. When we show up as ambassadors of Christ, the atmosphere shifts.

> We were never meant to change with the atmosphere. We are called to change the atmosphere.

We were never meant to change with the atmosphere. We are called to change the atmosphere. Many say, "You don't understand how hard it is at my school, or if you only knew my work environment." I may not have been to your school or work but one thing I do know—Jesus never allowed an atmosphere to shut Him up or change His ministry, because He understood who He was. The atmospheres of the world were never meant to change us but only for us to change them. So we must change the way we think and use the Word and our God-given examples of great men and women of the Bible. Moses and Jesus were in atmospheres where they were both wanted men. Instead of allowing those circumstances to change their atmospheres or ministry, they changed the atmospheres and brought many out from the kingdom of darkness into the Kingdom of Light. Let us now go and change the atmosphere by laying ourselves down as willing vessels of the Spirit of the living God.

The Atmosphere Shifted and He Didn't Even Know It

A friend of mine from a church I worked with in Atlanta, Georgia didn't really think going door to door was very effective. We put together an outreach where we would go visit all the visitors who had visited the church in the past six to twelve months. He didn't really want to participate, but he did because he wanted to support the outreach of the church. He decided to take a few young people with him. They visited three or four homes with no real success on the surface. One guy even yelled at them through the door quite rudely and told them to go away. This was a guy who had freely visited our church. They went home and didn't really think any more about it.

Later that day, my friend gets a telephone call. The man introduces himself as the guy who yelled at him through the door to get off of his porch. He was quite surprised to hear from him. He went on to apologize for being so rude and explained why he did not come to the door. He said that he was very embarrassed to see the youth there and didn't want them to see him. He said that he had been living in freedom from a gay lifestyle, but for the first time in a year he dressed up like a woman. When he saw who it was at the door, he was ashamed and convicted of his sin. He thanked him very much for coming by and let them know that God definitely used them in his life that day. He used that occurrence to get his attention and to encourage him to continue in his freedom from homosexuality.

They didn't feel the power of God at the door and felt it was pointless. No one sensed the breakthrough that was taking place behind the closed door. It didn't seem like God was moving at all. Little did they know, the entire atmosphere behind the door was changed. They couldn't see it, but God had used them to change the atmosphere from darkness to light.

The atmosphere shifts whether or not you see or feel it. Light can't be released without darkness fleeing.

We oftentimes will never know the effect and the atmospheric shift on the inside of someone until we make it to heaven. I believe that when we engage a lost person to reach them for Christ, if it were possible to see into the spiritual realm we would see angels and demons at war. As we approach a door of someone who is bound, we perhaps would see the whole area lighting up and darkness backing off. Whenever we engage someone going through a divorce; a child who is abused; a person who is addicted to drugs, porn, a false religion; a wife abused by her husband or whatever the case might be, I guarantee the atmosphere shifts whether or not you see or feel it. Light can't be released without darkness fleeing. Whenever a light comes on in a dark room, darkness flees. *"You are the light of the world. A town built on a hill cannot be hidden"* (Matt. 5:14). *"I am the light of the world. Whoever follows me will never walk in darkness, but will have the light of life"* (John 8:12). Whenever a child of God comes in contact with atmospheres and people bound in darkness, there is a fleeing and a shifting taking place in some form or fashion. It's a spiritual principle.

God, I ask You right now to release faith to shift atmospheres over communities, cities, regions, and even nations through our lives. Let us demolish every doubt and believe for breakthrough in this area. May we never again allow our abilities or inabilities to hold us back from allowing You to move in and through us. We ask You to speak to us right now over any atmosphere You want us to target and take our God-given authority as ambassadors and claim new territory for Your Kingdom.

I want to encourage you to take a moment now and allow God to speak and minister to you on how He wants you to walk this out in the days ahead. He doesn't want our "amens" but our actions.

Chapter 5

BAPTISM OF FIRE

Late one night in front of the Blue Planet Bar in Mobile, Alabama, a friend was arguing with this particular man concerning his need for Christ. They were going back and forth for quite some time. I've never argued anyone into the Kingdom of God. So I walked over and asked him a simple question, "Have you ever felt the power of God?" He wanted to, so I laid my hand upon him to pray after he gave me permission. I prayed a simple prayer: "God, touch him with the fire of the Holy Ghost!" He immediately felt the power of God and had a complete turn. He now wanted to receive Christ. When people feel the life-giving manifest presence of the Holy Spirit, it changes everything. I led him to Christ.

I laid hands on him again and the power of God fell a second time and he began to manifest devils. He bent over and literally began to throw up and foam right in front of everyone. A bouncer was standing right there as people were coming in and out of the bar. Many were walking by going from club to club. He was set free from demon possession right in the middle of enemy territory. *"But if it is by the Spirit of God that I drive out demons, then the kingdom of God has come upon you"* (Matt. 12:28). It wasn't in a church or crusade. It was in the middle of an area filled with bondage. That's the nature of God—to set the captive free no matter where you are (see Luke 4:18-19).

> When we partner with Jesus and walk in a fresh baptism of the Holy Spirit, we can and will walk in the miraculous power of God.

After he was set free, I prayed fire a third time. There was no need to change anything up. When I said it the third time, he doubled over and began to pray in tongues. None of us were praying in tongues. There was no way he would have responded in this way without God moving and especially with him not knowing about the baptism of the Holy Spirit. Jesus doesn't need anyone to have theology or understanding before He does the work. He's God and moves any way He likes. I asked him, "Have you ever heard that before?" He said, "No!" I prayed fire a fourth time. He doubled over yet again, opened his mouth and prayed in tongues a second time. I asked, "Have you done this before?" He said, "No!" It was amazing. He got saved, manifested devils, was set free, and got baptized in the Holy Spirit with the evidence of speaking in tongues in less than five minutes. It was a marvelous operation of being filled with the Holy Spirit and operating by His power. When we partner with Jesus and walk in a fresh baptism of the Holy Spirit, we can and will walk in the miraculous power of God.

In the day and hour that we live in, if there was ever a time for the church to walk in a fresh baptism of the Holy Spirit and fire, it's today. This could very well be the number-one need for the body of Christ in this hour. We will not witness spiritual transformation apart from the work of the Holy Spirit in and through us. We are, instead, witnessing the decline of the church's power, influence, and impact on society. If the church is ever to change society again, it must fully embrace the baptizing work of the Holy Spirit.

If there was ever an individual of whom it could be said that He didn't need the baptism of the Holy Spirit, it would be Jesus. Interestingly enough, before God allowed Jesus to face the greatest temptation of His life, He was baptized in the Spirit.

> *When all the people were being baptized, Jesus was baptized too. And as he was praying, heaven was opened and the Holy Spirit descended on him in bodily form like a dove. And a voice came from heaven: "You are my Son, whom I love; with you I am well pleased"* (Luke 3:21-22).

It was at this point that Jesus was filled with the Holy Spirit. *"Jesus, full of the Holy Spirit, left the Jordan and was led by the Spirit into the wilderness"* (Luke 4:1). If God knew that even Jesus, the perfect Son of God, needed the Holy Spirit to face the greatest temptation He would face to this point in His life, how much more do we as fallen humanity need the Holy Spirit? *A great deal more!*

Jesus was about to face off with the devil himself and needed the power that the Holy Spirit would minister to overcome the temptation of sin. The warfare and temptation that Jesus endured and overcame was so intense that God sent angels to attend to Him after it was over. *"Then the devil left him, and angels came and attended him"* (Matt. 4:11). The Holy Spirit empowered Jesus to endure the temptation and overcome. If Jesus needed the Holy Spirit to live a holy, victorious life, that is all the more reason that we do in our day as well—a day that is scarred by immorality, hate, and rebellion. If there was ever a time for the church to embrace the baptism of the Holy Spirit, it's today.

> If Jesus needed the Holy Spirit to live a holy, victorious life, that is all the more reason that we do in our day as well.

After overcoming the enemy in the desert, Jesus didn't just come out full of the Spirit but in the power of the Spirit. *"Jesus returned to Galilee in the power of the Spirit, and news about him spread through the whole countryside"* (Luke 4:14). It's not enough to be filled alone; we must walk in the power of the Spirit. We are filled for our sake but endued with power for the world's sake. Jesus didn't just walk around filled and full of joy, though this is fruit that we should have. He walked about moving and demonstrating that He was baptized in power. Out of every message Jesus could have delivered, according to Luke, for His first preaching address to the world, God moved Him to articulate a foundational theology on the operation of the Holy Spirit through His life and the lives of the believers who would soon follow. He could have spoken on hundreds of topics, but God felt this would be the most important way to start His preaching ministry.

The Spirit of the Lord is on me, because he has anointed me to proclaim good news to the poor. He has sent me to proclaim freedom for the prisoners and recovery of sight for the blind, to set the oppressed free, to proclaim the year of the Lord's favor (Luke 4:18-19).

This would be such a foundation of His ministry. He wanted everyone from the Jew to the Gentile, and everyone in between, to know why the Holy Spirit was upon Him and how it would operate. We see that it is a work of power to the lost and broken. The Holy Spirit empowers us to primarily minister and break the hell off of people. His work is for us to destroy every yoke, oppression, and bondage of darkness. He empowers us to preach in a dimension of power that would be impossible without Him.

> The Holy Spirit empowers us to primarily minister and break the hell off of people. His work is for us to destroy every yoke, oppression, and bondage of darkness.

This shows us that it was the empowerment of the Holy Spirit and the anointing at work in and through Jesus that released the miraculous. Jesus didn't heal the sick or raise the dead out of His perfection or divinity. He paved the way as an example to follow. No human is perfect or divine. Therefore, if this was how Jesus moved in power, we are hopeless to be imitators of Christ in this area. We see in Philippians the apostle Paul laid a great foundation for this monumental truth.

Who, being in very nature God, did not consider equality with God something to be used to his own advantage; rather, he made himself nothing by taking the very nature of a servant, being made in human likeness. And being found in appearance as a man, he humbled himself by becoming obedient to death, even death on a cross! (Philippians 2:6-8)

It is clear that Christ did not hold, grasp, or use His equality with God to His own advantage in any aspect. He left it behind. He took on the nature of a servant. Servants are not divine. He was made human. Humans have zero divinity. They will never be equal to God in any shape, form, or fashion. That was the downfall of Satan; he tried to be an equal to God and it didn't work out too well for him. Jesus took on the appearance of a man and became obedient to death, even death on a cross. If there was ever an act of humility, this was it. The divine God put on flesh, left His divinity, and became obedient to the most humiliating form of death reserved for the worst of society. Jesus, the Son of God, is truly amazing to do this for mankind.

Therefore, when Jesus stepped forward and commanded Lazarus to come out of the tomb and be raised from the dead, this was not performed by His divinity.

Jesus called in a loud voice, "Lazarus, come out!" The dead man came out, his hands and feet wrapped with strips of linen, and a cloth around his face. Jesus said to them, "Take off the grave clothes and let him go" (John 11:43-44).

This miracle was performed by faith through the baptism of the Holy Spirit. It was the Holy Spirit Himself who took those words of faith and blew death back and released life into the dead corpse. This was a prime example of Christ ministering through the baptism of the Spirit.

Again, when Jesus spoke these words to a blind beggar, *"Receive your sight; your faith has healed you,"* the scriptures tell us that *"immediately he received his sight and followed Jesus, praising God. When all the people saw it, they also praised God"* (Luke 18:42-43). Jesus, working through the baptism of the Holy Spirit by faith, healed the sick. This is a freeing truth to many. *We do not have to be divine to move in the fullness of the Spirit.* Jesus said we would do even greater works than He did and gave us the example of how it would work. He would not have asked us to follow Him if He did this in His divinity because He would've known we would never be divine. He did, however, know we would soon have access to the same power that He was ministering in and through. He understood that in just a short time, this great manifestation of the Holy Spirit was going to be poured out on earth for all mankind for the first time in history. He showed us how one operates in the fullness of the Spirit— then He released this power upon the earth.

> We do not have to be divine to move in the fullness of the Spirit.

Fire from Heaven

Jesus would soon be crucified after a powerful ministry. During His arrest and crucifixion, many of His closest friends and disciples fled. These were not awful men; they didn't want to flee. They just could not understand why everything was happening the way it was and their hero was now being beaten and would be taken out. Even Peter denied he knew Christ:

> *And when some there had kindled a fire in the middle of the courtyard and had sat down together, Peter sat down with them. A servant girl saw him seated there in the firelight. She looked closely at him and said, "This man was with him." But he denied it. "Woman, I don't know him," he said* (Luke 22:55-57).

Moments earlier, Peter cut a man's ear off in attempt to protect Christ, but now he denied he even knew Him. Fear had baptized his heart. He wasn't evil. It just wasn't supposed to happen this way in his mind. How was everything going to come to pass? The man he had just spent three years of his life devoted to was about to die, and he didn't want to join him. Peter fled in fear.

Jesus died and arose from the dead on the third day. He gathered His disciples to Himself and had a two-point message for forty days. Everything Jesus ever said was absolute truth. What would His final message be? He would conclude in a similar fashion to the way He started—the baptism of the Holy Spirit—and the point He added was *win souls and make disciples.* Jesus finished every Gospel with this theme and started Acts with it as well:

> *All authority in heaven and on earth has been given to me. Therefore go and make disciples of all nations, baptizing them in the name of the Father and of the Son and of the Holy Spirit, and teaching them to obey*

everything I have commanded you. And surely I am with you always, to the very end of the age (Matthew 28:18-20).

Go into all the world and preach the gospel to all creation. Whoever believes and is baptized will be saved, but whoever does not believe will be condemned. And these signs will accompany those who believe: In my name they will drive out demons; they will speak in new tongues; they will pick up snakes with their hands; and when they drink deadly poison, it will not hurt them at all; they will place their hands on sick people, and they will get well (Mark 16:15-18).

Peace be with you! As the Father has sent me, I am sending you (John 20:21).

I am going to send you what my Father has promised; but stay in the city until you have been clothed with power from on high (Luke 24:49).

But you will receive power when the Holy Spirit comes on you; and you will be my witnesses in Jerusalem, and in all Judea and Samaria, and to the ends of the earth (Acts 1:8).

Jesus did not want them to be confused about their assignment. It was very clear and can be summed up in two points without getting too deep: Be filled with the Holy Spirit to be empowered to move in signs and wonders and win the lost. It seems that many churches and Christians have lost this simple assignment and that we're focused on everything but these two points. Many things have bogged us down and we've lost focus of our primary assignment. So many are going after the next revelation or move when Jesus has never moved from His last statements.

> So many are going after the next revelation or move when Jesus has never moved from His last statements.

He told His disciples to shut everything down until they were filled with the Holy Spirit. What would the church look like today if this were our main priority? He didn't want them preaching, laying hands on the sick, building churches, or distributing food to the needy. He wanted them to go and tarry until they were baptized with the Holy Ghost and fire. Only after thoroughly communicating this did He ascend into heaven.

This is a real insight when preaching the Gospel and it is how Christ directed it to be done. Realize this was the first time in the history of mankind since sin was made manifest through the fall of man, that man could be redeemed through the completed work of Christ. Jesus had just taken the judgment we deserved for our sin and we could now be redeemed by His blood and receive salvation. You could not be saved and fully cleansed from your sins until the sacrifice of Christ was made and His blood was shed. The blood of bulls and goats did not have saving power. So for the first time in history, one of the disciples could stand and preach the Gospel, give a call for repentance, and people could be saved. That's why Christ died and is as ready as He was that day to see people saved. He knew for the word to be effective the way He intended, it needed to be saturated, dipped, and baptized in the Holy Spirit. That's the formula for preachers and the witnesses of the Gospel of Jesus Christ. Jesus didn't want the Gospel to go forth on its own; He wanted the fire of the Holy Spirit to be upon the message and the vessel it comes through. He was saying the Gospel has one temperature—burning hot. After communicating this truth over and over, He would ascend to the right hand of the Father.

The Gospel has one temperature— burning hot.

Now the disciples would wait for the promised Holy Spirit to come and baptize them all. They would soon receive. After ten days of waiting, they were all filled with the Spirit and began to speak in other tongues. Each individual received a flame of fire that appeared as a tongue of fire on their head (see Acts 2:1–4). What would take place next would shake Jerusalem, impact the entire globe, and change the course of history.

> *When they heard this sound, a crowd came together in bewilderment, because each one heard their own language being spoken. Utterly amazed, they asked: "Aren't all these who are speaking Galileans? Then how is it that each of us hears them in our native language?" (Acts 2:6-8)*

The crowd was totally blown away at the manifestation of the Spirit. When was the last time church was released on a Sunday and the town was bewildered and utterly amazed? This should be the bar. Not just a service where God shows up, but where

He shows up and we in turn impact the world. This should be our prayer and the ache of our soul to happen in every city in the world that has a church in it. This is what happens when there are ten straight days of prayer. What would happen if your church brought its core together and there were ten days of fasting and prayer? Who knows; you may step out and your entire city stand utterly amazed.

The disciples knew what Jesus said (now recorded in Luke 4 and at the end of the Gospels) and were fully prepared. Preach and move in miraculous power. *"The Spirit of the Lord is on me, because he has anointed me to proclaim good news to the poor"* (Luke 4:18). Peter then stood up and began to address the crowd. Don't kid yourself; Peter was fully aware of the atmosphere and notoriety of Jesus—they had just crucified Him. The devil followed Peter all the way up to that point of preaching and probably reminded him that the very ones who crucified Christ were in the crowd. I can hear the devil whisper in Peter's ear, "They killed Him and they will kill you if you utter one word." He didn't listen, but proclaimed:

> *This man was handed over to you by God's deliber-*
> *ate plan and foreknowledge; and you, with the help*
> *of wicked men, put him to death by nailing him to*
> *the cross. ...God has made this Jesus, whom you cru-*
> *cified, both Lord and Messiah* (Acts 2:23, 36).

Not only were the ones who shouted for Him to be crucified in the crowd, but it seems as if some of the ones that participated in the execution were present as well. The devil was sure to let Peter know this.

Fire Deep Down in Your Bones

Weeks earlier Peter had fled in fear, but now, *filled with the Spirit*, he overcame his fear. Though the occasion may warrant fear, you are filled with the Overcomer, and His fire is more powerful and intense than the fear that tries to suppress. I love the example in the Old Testament with Jeremiah.

> But if I say, "I will not mention his word or speak anymore in his name," his word is in my heart like a fire, a fire shut up in my bones. I am weary of holding it in; indeed, I cannot (Jeremiah 20:9).

The context of Jeremiah making this particular declaration, "His word is like a fire in my bones," was not in a nice church or just preaching on the street corner. He was in an area that was in direct opposition to God's Word. On top of that, he had just been severely beaten and imprisoned.

> When the priest Pashhur son of Immer, the official in charge of the temple of the Lord, heard Jeremiah prophesying these things, he had Jeremiah the prophet beaten and put in the stocks at the Upper Gate of Benjamin at the Lord's temple (Jeremiah 20:1-2).

He was broken up, possibly suffering broken ribs, black eyes, and a bloody face, just for starters. If there was ever a time he should hold back and heal, it was then. He wouldn't! The fire that was shut up in his bones was more real and intense than his beating. God, send that fire once again! In the church world today, most believers don't even share their faith in a safe place with no persecution that would cause bodily harm. What did he have that most of the church needs? Fire in our bones!

> In the church world today, most believers don't even share their faith in a safe place with no persecution that would cause bodily harm. What did he have that most of the church needs? Fire in our bones!

Peter didn't mince words either. He called out those who were living in rebellion toward God and called them to repent. His word had so much power on it, *"When the people heard this, they were cut to the heart and said to Peter and the other apostles, 'Brothers, what shall we do?'"* (Acts 2:37). After they asked this question, Peter didn't ask them to repeat a prayer after him. He told them to repent. *"Peter replied, 'Repent and be baptized, every one of you, in the name of Jesus Christ for the forgiveness of your sins. And you will receive the gift of the Holy Spirit'"* (Acts 2:38). This is what our world is in desperate need of today! Unashamed firebrands who will unabashedly stand and preach the full counsel of God, holding not one point back and being so full of faith and God's Spirit that entire cities are cut to the heart! May the early Christians' determination and exploits encourage us to raise the bar and cry out for a fresh baptism of the Holy Ghost and fire.

Perpetually Filled/Fresh Baptism

After the baptism of the Spirit, we need to be refilled on a continual basis. Peter was filled in Acts 2 and saw the first 3,000 enter into the Kingdom through his preaching. Not long after, he was used powerfully to see a man crippled since birth healed by the power of God (see Acts 3). Then shortly after, he and John were jailed for using the name of Jesus (see Acts 4:3). Persecution had broken out against them for using the name of Jesus. They were reprimanded and told not to use the name of Jesus any more. The stakes just got higher, and now they would have to make a choice to back off and tone it down or obey God, ramp it up, and move forward. What would happen?

> *On their release, Peter and John went back to their own people and reported all that the chief priests and the elders had said to them. When they heard this, they raised their voices together in prayer to God. "Sovereign Lord," they said, "you made the heavens and the earth and the sea, and everything in them"* (Acts 4:23-24).

> *"Now, Lord, consider their threats and enable your servants to speak your word with great boldness. Stretch out your hand to heal and perform signs and wonders through the name of your holy servant Jesus." After they prayed, the place where they were meeting was shaken. And they were all filled with the Holy Spirit and spoke the word of God boldly* (Acts 4:29-31).

They didn't back off one inch. They did what we all should do in the face of direct opposition—cry out to God.

They didn't back off one inch. They did what we all should do in the face of direct opposition—cry out to God. They were clearly shaken and weren't quite sure what to do or how to handle the situation. The Holy Spirit would give them renewed strength, infusion, and a fresh filling. They were initially baptized weeks earlier but needed a fresh infilling to move forward. If they were not continually filled, they would have ended up like most of the church in our times—neutralized, little impact, politically correct, and muzzled. This was not the case; they received a fresh baptism. What was the result? They "spoke the word of God *boldly.*" This is a clear indicator of a fresh baptism—you speak the word of God boldly and fearlessly, with no regard to the threats of the spirit of this age. Many have experienced Acts 2, the initial baptism, but we aren't walking in a fresh baptism as the disciples perpetually walked in. *God, we need an Acts 4 experience* as the body of Christ. Send the fire again!

God, we ask You right now to baptize us afresh in the fire of the Holy Spirit. We ask You to so submerge us in Your river of liquid fire that not only will Christians feel the heat of Your presence on us, but Buddhists, Muslims, atheists, witches, addicts, and all who are away from You would declare that something of the divine is upon us. Lord, we make this the bar we will believe for.

Chapter 6

IT'S TIME TO PROPHESY

like old Mustangs. If I could buy a 1969 Mustang with low mileage in mint condition, that would be a tremendous find—*at the right price, I must say.* Let's suppose the price has been discussed and we are in complete agreement. I walk to the car and take a closer look. I'm taken aback by the superb condition that it's in. It has the original chrome wheels from the manufacturer; I take a seat on the driver's side and everything is original down to the eight-track cassette player with Elvis's Christmas hits coming out of the deck. I ask the owner for the keys to give it a test spin, but the owner says, "There is just one problem: there is no motor in the car." It looked good and everything seemed right, but the source of power was absent. The power that moved the car was not there. The outside appeared normal, but the car had no power. This is the condition of many churches *and Christians.* Everything is taking place as normal, but when you look under the hood, the power is gone. One of the most devastating attacks on the church in this past century was the removal of the power of God operating in believers.

If the enemy cannot get you to fall into sin, he will try to get you to settle for less. Paul said we should eagerly desire spiritual gifts, especially the gift of prophecy. *"Follow the way of love and eagerly desire gifts of the Spirit, especially prophecy"* (1 Cor. 14:1). The gifts of the Spirit will not just pop out of heaven willy-nilly. God has called us to seek them. Just take a look inside and ask yourself this question: *Is the reason I am not flowing in the gifts of the Spirit because I have not cried out to God for them?* God is not calling us to just dedicate a season of prayer for the gifts. He wants it to be a lifestyle of crying out for these powerful gifts to manifest in our lives. For too long we have settled for less and have not pressed in for a breakthrough in this area. Paul takes it one step further. "Desire all the gifts, but especially the gift of prophecy." This gift is the one gift that can open the hearts of individuals in an amazing way (see 1 Cor. 14:24-25).

> Is the reason I am not flowing in the gifts of the Spirit because I have not cried out to God for them?

I've heard the question posed many times, "Why don't we see the power of God as in days past?" One simple response is to ask if we are following the divine directions. Sometimes when simple instructions from God's Word are overlooked, it can short-circuit the whole process. Everything can be in working order in a powerful automobile, but if key crucial fuses are blown, it will cause the power in that car to cease from operating. Prayer to operate in the gifts of the Spirit may seem small, but if not followed through, it can short-circuit the move of the supernatural in one's life.

A Vision, a Prophecy, and a Demonstration of Power

One morning while I was in Pueblo, Colorado mobilizing a church in evangelism, I was praying in my hotel room before the pastor was going to pick me up for lunch. Toward the end of my time in prayer I began to intercede for the waitress who would serve us that day for lunch. I was putting First Corinthians 14:1 into practice. I earnestly asked God to give me a word, but instead He gave me a vision of what she would look like.

He spoke to me that this young lady had been very hurt by a male father figure in her life. This person she loved very much had hurt her tremendously. God began to describe to me the kind of personality she had and the soft heart He had given her. He spoke to me about how the hurt caused from this man hurt so much that her loving and tender heart had become callused and unable to receive love from anyone, including God. This was hurting God's heart because He wanted to comfort her with His love, but couldn't. He wanted to minister healing and life to the damage done to her heart so that she could receive love from Him.

When we arrived at the restaurant and our waitress walked away from our table, I told the pastor what had happened that morning. It was the exact person I saw in my vision. I told him I would wait until the end of our meal and tell her what I felt to tell her. When the bill came, I left a $20 tip, which was more than 50 percent of the bill. (Believers can never go wrong blessing people in some form or fashion before they minister to them.)

When she came back to our table, I asked her for a few minutes. I then proceeded to tell her that I was praying for her that morning and that I saw her in a vision. I told her God gave me a word for her. Then I delivered the word He gave me. She looked at me and was stunned. God had completely read her mail. She had been hurt deeply by the individual I described and could no longer receive love from a man. She had never experienced anything like this before in her life.

She looked at me totally puzzled as she wondered how on earth I knew this. I explained how God showed me this and that He loved her so much that it broke His heart that she couldn't receive love from Him. I asked her if she had ever received Christ as her personal Savior and she never had. I asked her if she would like to, and without hesitation she said yes. We led her to Christ for the first time in her life. I didn't have to convince her Jesus was real. She experienced His power firsthand. She immediately went over and began to testify to her manager about what had just happened. Within five minutes, she was testifying of the goodness of God.

The very next day I was out on a baseball field participating in an outreach with the church to the community. During this time an individual introduced me to his stepdaughter. I wouldn't find out until later that she worked at the same restaurant as the girl from the day before in my vision. All of a sudden, I began to get a prophetic word for her as well. I laid hands on her and she was hit by the power of God and fell out right in the dirt under God's manifest presence. There were no catchers or worship teams setting the atmosphere; the power of God just hit her.

We began to minister deliverance as she shook on the ground in the dirt. God began a powerful work in her and she came to church the next night.

That night she repented of her sin. I didn't know until after the service that she had invited another friend from that same restaurant. Her friend must have come in late because they were not sitting together. I ministered to her friend sitting somewhere else, and she was also hit by the power. From my remembrance, this was the first time anything like this had ever happened to her. I led her to Christ as well.

After a time of crying out for the prophetic to operate in my life and stepping out in what I felt God saying, three girls from the same restaurant turned toward God. If we follow God's Word and take a step of faith, He is faithful to show His love and presence. He is just looking for people to work with His mission in touching a lost and hurting world.

The Master at Work

The Gospel of John describes an instance of how Jesus operated in the prophetic. Let's take a look at some valuable insights on how Jesus set this woman up to receive as He followed what God was saying and doing:

> *So he came to a town in Samaria called Sychar, near the plot of ground Jacob had given to his son Joseph. Jacob's well was there, and Jesus, tired as he was from the journey, sat down by the well. It was about noon. When a Samaritan woman came to draw water, Jesus said to her, "Will you give me a drink?" (His disciples had gone into the town to buy food.) The*

Samaritan woman said to him, "You are a Jew and I am a Samaritan woman. How can you ask me for a drink?" (For Jews do not associate with Samaritans.) (John 4:5-9).

The woman was amazed that Jesus asked for a drink. Jews would avoid Samaritans at all costs, so she was especially amazed that a Jew would humble Himself and ask her for a drink. This is a good point in reaching people with God's love—find a way to humble yourself to whomever you are talking with. He will give more grace. The Bible says: *"God resists the proud, but gives grace to the humble"* (James 4:6 NKJV). Jesus came to her in humility—not pride. If He had come in pride, God (and the woman) would have resisted Him, but because of the humility He walked in, it was a door opener for the grace of God to saturate their conversation. He opened up heaven, and now the grace of God would be on everything said. Humility makes reaching people much easier.

> Find a way to humble yourself to whomever you are talking with. Humility makes reaching people much easier.

I have missed this powerful truth of humility in one-on-one evangelism many times. You can come to someone with the right heart, motive, and passion, and still completely miss it. God can still use you, but it is a big help when we go in humility. Having pride about the fact that we have the truth and everyone else doesn't is a terrible attitude. Our knowledge of truth should be communicated in grace, not pride. We need the gift of discernment to know when to speak the truth in boldness and when to speak with gentleness. James 4:6 gives us a powerful principle in connecting with people who don't know Christ. Oftentimes we will apply principles like this one in many aspects of our lives but not in reaching people. Use this simple foundation as you are in conversations with people who need Jesus, and watch how His presence begins to move and His grace covers the conversation.

When this woman asked Jesus the question, *"You are a Jew and I am a Samaritan woman. How can You ask me for a drink?"* He did not even address it. This could have led their conversation down a road that would not have borne fruit. Jesus discerned that the question she asked was not a point God was dealing with at that time. I have missed it many times and found myself sidetracked from what God wanted me to focus on or talk about at that particular time. Timing is critical in evangelism. This is why it is crucial to ask God every day for discernment in how to communicate the Gospel in each situation. Jesus discerned by the Holy Spirit to go in a different direction and recognized that the question she asked was a ploy of the devil to completely sidetrack the conversation. How was Jesus able to do this? Because He had developed a communicative relationship with the Father:

> Very truly I tell you, the Son can do nothing by himself; he can do only what he sees his Father doing, because whatever the Father does the Son also does (John 5:19).

Through prayer and listening to God, the Holy Spirit will develop this powerful ability in you as well.

This is the ultimate place and level any believer can walk in to reach people for Christ. There is no better way than to do what God is doing and say what God is saying. This doesn't happen overnight, and we shouldn't get discouraged if we engage an unbeliever and don't sense God speaking through us. However, when connecting with the lost, we must *always* have our spiritual eyes and ears open throughout the whole conversation for what God is saying and doing. That is the bar—period. As we develop and move in this principle, we will do more than randomly reaching the lost, but will have a front-row seat as soul after soul is healed, touched, delivered, and brought into God's gracious gift of salvation.

> When connecting with the lost, we must **always** have our spiritual eyes and ears open throughout the whole conversation for what God is saying and doing. That is the bar—period.

Jesus's conversation with the woman at the well continues:

> *Jesus answered her, "If you knew the gift of God and who it is that asks you for a drink, you would have asked him and he would have given you living water." "Sir," the woman said, "you have nothing to draw with and the well is deep. Where can you get this living water? Are you greater than our father Jacob, who gave us the well and drank from it himself, as did also his sons and his livestock?" Jesus answered,*

"Everyone who drinks this water will be thirsty again, but whoever drinks the water I give them will never thirst. Indeed, the water I give them will become in them a spring of water welling up to eternal life." The woman said to him, "Sir, give me this water so that I won't get thirsty and have to keep coming here to draw water" (John 4:10-15).

She asked Him another religious question. "Where can You get this living water? Are You greater than our father Jacob, who gave us the well and drank from it himself, as did also his sons and his flocks and herds?" Again, Jesus did not answer her question. He took the conversation in a totally different direction for the second time. Jesus knew that He was greater than Jacob, but if He had spoken that truth at this particular time it could have offended her. This woman may have walked away without hearing another word Jesus had to say. Jesus knew that the Spirit had not yet moved on her heart and she was not yet ready to receive this truth. After God moves on a heart, it is a much better time to deal with something that might be controversial or confrontational.

As we see yet again when we engage with unbelievers just as Jesus did in this passage, there are immediately two plans set in motion for the conversation. God's plan and the devil's plan. This is why it is imperative to develop an ear to what God is saying. Oftentimes in my experience, when people ask questions they often aren't looking for an answer but rather an argument.

For example, I've been asked questions like this: "If God is real, why are people dying of water pollution in the nation of Mozambique?" The response could be, "That's amazing that you would ask that question. I just did an internship for six months there studying as part of my master's degree in biology and ecology. We actually ran tests on the river systems of that nation. We found that the reason people were dying had nothing to do with nature's involvement, nor God for that matter. In the vast number of deaths, our finding confirmed that other nations in direct contact with Mozambique were dumping nuclear waste in their rivers, which was causing people to die. It was actually radiation poison caused by man and had nothing to do with God." Then without even listening they may say, "Well, if God is real, then why do people have AIDS?" They're not looking for an answer, but an argument. At those moments, it's time to remember Paul's words:

> For our struggle is not against flesh and blood, but against the rulers, against the authorities, against the powers of this dark world and against the spiritual forces of evil in the heavenly realms (Ephesians 6:12).

I have fallen prey to these arguments many times in the past and realized that it bears little to no fruit. It's simply better to identify the questions that are meant to divert, distract, and provoke an argument. They don't line up with God's plan for the conversation, so simply don't address them. To the best of your ability, follow what God is saying and doing, and keep the conversation going in the direction of the Gospel. Oftentimes these distractions take the focus off of the individual's need for Christ, so always be alert to this trap.

Jesus kept the focus on ministering eternal life to her. She thought He had some kind of new water or invention to quench the natural thirst for water forever. This sounded great to her because she would no longer need to get water for herself. She wanted this kind of water. She took what Jesus was saying literally and applied it to the natural man, not the spiritual man.

> Jesus kept the focus on
> ministering eternal life.

Jesus continues to engage the woman: *"'Go, call your husband and come back.' 'I have no husband,' she replied. Jesus said to her, 'You are right when you say you have no husband. The fact is, you have had five husbands, and the man you now have is not your husband. What you have just said is quite true'"* (John 4:16–18). For the third time in a row, Jesus did not respond to what she had just said. "Sir, give me this water so that I won't get thirsty and have to keep coming here to draw water." Instead, His response was, "Go, call your husband and come back." She finally agreed to take some water in her own understanding and Jesus completely ignored it. How wild is that? How many people would think you were listening to them if you seemed to ignore everything they said? That is what it looked like Jesus was doing. He was listening to the Father and said what He heard the Father say. John 14:10 says, *"Don't you believe that I am in the Father, and that the Father is in me? The words I say to you I do not speak on my own authority. Rather, it is the Father, living in me, who is doing his work."* John 5:19-20 says, *"Very truly I tell you, the Son can do nothing by himself; he can do only what he sees his Father doing, because whatever the Father does the Son also does. For the Father loves the Son and shows him all he does. Yes, and he will show him even greater works than these, so that you will be amazed."*

Jesus was now beginning to operate in a prophetic gifting when He said, "Go, call your husband and come back." He knew the answer to the question before He ever asked it. He was looking for repentance, but she tried to avoid the question. She said, "I have no husband." That would lead Him to believe she was a widow or that she was never married. We need the prophetic gifts to help us see what only God sees.

Her reply, "I have no husband," was a smoke screen meant to deceive Jesus. These smoke screens people put up desperately require the operation of the prophetic. Jesus saw right through it. How many times have you talked to someone about Jesus and were told, "Yeah, I go to church," but you knew the person was not right with God? This is where a word of knowledge can be powerful and life changing.

> Just because we have a prophetic word or truth does not mean we immediately confront people with it. We must learn to do it in love as Christ so beautifully shows us.

Jesus responded with a word of knowledge and told her just what was going on. Jesus may well have known the whole time He was ministering to her what she was involved in and could have blasted her with a prophetic word when they first met. This is a very good point to examine. Just because we have a prophetic word or truth does not mean we immediately confront people with it. We must learn to do it in love as Christ so beautifully shows us. Jesus spent time connecting with her and talking with her before He gave her this word. The Bible says:

> *If I speak in the tongues of men or of angels, but do not have love, I am only a resounding gong or a clanging cymbal. If I have the gift of prophecy and can fathom all mysteries and all knowledge, and if I have a faith that can move mountains, but do not have love, I am nothing. If I give all I possess to the poor and give over my body to hardship that I may boast, but do not have love, I gain nothing* (1 Corinthians 13:1-3).

Jesus did something at this point that seems to be more politically and socially incorrect now than in days past. He dealt with her sin. Jesus understood that if she was going to enter into the Kingdom of God, He had to deal with her sin. This can be uncomfortable at times, but we must not shrink back from addressing sin that will keep people from entering heaven.

> *Or do you not know that wrongdoers will not inherit the kingdom of God? Do not be deceived: Neither the sexually immoral nor idolaters nor adulterers nor men who have sex with men nor thieves nor the greedy nor drunkards nor slanderers nor swindlers will inherit the kingdom of God* (1 Corinthians 6:9-10).

It is much more unloving to ignore these areas than it is to reveal the truth. "*Then you will know the truth, and the truth will set you free*" (John 8:32). When we interact with people in these areas with love and a pure heart, we're not responsible for the way people react. Our primary responsibility is to minister the whole truth and counsel of God.

You Don't Learn That in Bible School

One day while meeting some pastor friends for lunch at a local restaurant, I felt led to stand up and preach. I have a quick, 30-second exhortation that I give in these situations. It's very simple; I say, "Hello my name is Joe Oden, and I have an announcement to make. I serve Jesus Christ and if there is anyone here who is sick, addicted, or depressed, I would love to pray for you and believe Jesus Christ will set you free." After I had finished doing this that day I sat down and nothing really happened. I felt a bit dumb.

Then God gave me part number two. How many of you would be fired up to give part number two if part number one didn't seem to work? It was a real wild word. I felt Him say, "Your waitress is living in sexual sin with her boyfriend and I want you to rebuke her." *Wow!* I didn't really want to do that. However, this is biblical. The word plainly tells us, *"Preach the word; be prepared in season and out of season; correct, rebuke and encourage—with great patience and careful instruction"* (2 Tim. 4:2). Two-thirds of this passage is for ministers to be corrective and one-third encouraging.

Feeling a bit nervous to tell the female waitress this, I asked one of the pastors I was sitting with who was around 70 years of age. I knew he was full of wisdom and would tell me if I should proceed with this word. Without hesitation he replied, "You had better obey God." After he said that, I knew I had to deliver that word. But how was I going to tell this young lady whom I'd never met that she needed to repent of living in sexual sin? They didn't teach me how to do that in Bible school.

> How was I going to tell this young lady whom I'd never met that she needed to repent of living in sexual sin? They didn't teach me how to do that in Bible school.

When she walked up to the table to ask if we needed anything else, I asked her a question that I felt would open up the door. I asked, "If Jesus walked up to you right now, what would He say?" She smiled kindly and said, "He'd ask me for a glass of sweet tea." I thought that was pretty quick witted. Then I said, "Or He might say that you're living in sexual sin with your boyfriend and that you need to repent." I then went on to prophetically tell her the emotions and heartache she was living in and under in this relationship.

She didn't get mad at all. Her eyes began to fill with tears and she got down on her knees and began to get right with God and committed to end the ungodly relationship. She got on her knees in front of her manager and the whole restaurant. When she got up, she looked at me and asked, "Who are you and what do you do?" She knew it was God who had revealed this to me, and I didn't need to convince her that God was real because she just had an encounter with His love and presence.

Many think they could never do something like this and that people would get mad and think you were judgmental. More often than not, if the word is given in love, they receive it and are impacted by God. God used Nathan in Second Samuel 12 to rebuke David for hidden sexual sin and murder. God will often use the prophetic to call people to repentance. When received, it turns the heart of sinful men back to a right relationship with a loving God. If used correctly, it will save people from the eternal punishment of hell.

I spoke to this young lady about a year later. She was in church every Sunday morning and Sunday night. God used me to reset the course of her life and God can use you to do the same. You just have to pray earnestly as Paul has directed us and take a step of faith and watch God do the rest.

> People will listen to you if God touches them before you speak to them. God can and will develop this form of touching the lost in you if you will be patient and diligent in prayer and obedient in stepping out and not get ahead of God or behind Him.

John continues the exchange: *"'Sir,' the woman said, 'I can see that you are a prophet. Our ancestors worshiped on this mountain, but you Jews claim that the place where we must worship is in Jerusalem'"* (John 4:19-20). Through this word of knowledge, she now knew at the very least that Jesus was a prophet sent from God. He connected her heart to the heart of God. That is one of the most beautiful forms of evangelism that can ever take place—to connect the heart of someone who is not a Christian to the heart of God. When this takes place, what you may think is confrontational will more often than not be received. Now Jesus could address all the questions she had and speak directly with her. She was now ready to receive what He had to say because the Spirit of God had touched her. People will listen to you if God touches them before you speak to them. God can and will develop this form of touching the lost in you if you will be patient and diligent in prayer and obedient in stepping out and not get ahead of God or behind Him.

Jesus replied to the woman and finally revealed to her His true identity:

> *"Woman," Jesus replied, "believe me, a time is coming when you will worship the Father neither on this mountain nor in Jerusalem. You Samaritans worship what you do not know; we worship what we do know, for salvation is from the Jews. Yet a time is coming and has now come when the true worshipers will worship the Father in the Spirit and in truth, for they are the kind of worshipers the Father seeks. God is spirit, and his worshipers must worship in the Spirit and in truth." The woman said, "I know that Messiah" (called Christ) "is coming. When he comes, he will explain everything to us." Then Jesus declared, "I, the one speaking to you—I am he"* (John 4:21-26).

Jesus was now able to proclaim her need for salvation and call her to turn and follow Him. He addressed the fact that she was religious and worshiped what she did not know. This truth could have offended her at the beginning of the conversation. Jesus listened to the Father and when He felt it was right to expose this matter, He did. She might never have received His word if He had given it to her before she had an experience with God. He finished the conversation by telling her that He was the Messiah, *the way of salvation*. It's instructive that the very statement we often begin with is the statement that Jesus ended with.

John 4 shows us that we have a great opportunity to touch people with a prophetic anointing that will reveal who Jesus is. This woman not only was radically transformed but became a witness and began to evangelize immediately. Look what happens as a result of this woman's encounter with Christ:

> *Many of the Samaritans from that town believed in him because of the woman's testimony, "He told me everything I ever did." So when the Samaritans came to him, they urged him to stay with them, and he stayed two days. And because of his words many more became believers. They said to the woman, "We no longer believe just because of what you said; now we have heard for ourselves, and we know that this man really is the Savior of the world" (John 4:39-42).*

Some might say this Samaritan woman became the very first female evangelist. You never know if the person you touch might be the one to win the city. In that sense, when you are witnessing to one person, you are witnessing to an entire city—at the very least, to that person's friends, family, co-workers, and neighbors. Jesus was obedient to minister to one woman at a well, and God used it to touch the whole city. If Jesus would have offended her, He could have lost the whole city. Through God's grace and a word of knowledge that was ministered in love, a city was touched.

> Through God's grace and a word
> of knowledge that was ministered
> in love, a city was touched.

The next time you pass through a small town, be perceptive of that light nudge from the Holy Spirit to speak of Jesus to that waitress or clerk or cashier. You never know who they might influence—perhaps the whole town!

Taking That First Step

When God deals with me in the prophetic, it's not an audible voice or an exact sentence from God. It's often in strong impressions. I then use the faith God has given me and step out. Often, I will say something like this, "My name is Joe and I am a Christian and was just praying for you and felt God wanted me to tell you..." I don't end it with a, "Thus saith the Lord." I will usually ask, "Does what I just said bear witness with you?" That does two things. One, it lets you know if you're being led properly. If you missed it, you can tell the person you were doing your best to follow God's lead and don't want to speak for God if you're off.

If you miss it, God is not sitting in heaven waiting to strike you down. If you step out in the right spirit and motive and your heart is truly to bring glory to God and salvation to the lost, He will be happy and help you where you've missed it. Just as you develop other skills, it takes time. After time and practice, you become more seasoned and know when it's Him. But you will never become more seasoned if you don't take the first step and put yourself out there.

I have two young children. The first time they took a step, guess what happened? They fell down. I didn't yell or discipline them. I celebrated their first steps even though it wasn't perfect. Then, we continued to work with them and encourage them. That's the way God is. He understands our limitations and shortfalls as we endeavor to do His work. He will continue to encourage us and help us along the way. So don't let fear hold you back. Pray earnestly for the gift of prophecy, as Paul exhorted us, then step out and prophesy life into a lost and hurting world.

The Calling of Nathanael—Why Argue? Just Connect Them to Jesus

The Gospel of John also describes an instance of how one believer interacted with an unbeliever to connect him to Christ and both became His disciples:

> *The next day Jesus decided to leave for Galilee. Finding Philip, he said to him, "Follow me." Philip, like Andrew and Peter, was from the town of Bethsaida. Philip found Nathanael and told him, "We have found the one Moses wrote about in the Law, and about whom the prophets also wrote— Jesus of Nazareth, the son of Joseph." "Nazareth! Can anything good come from there?" Nathanael asked. "Come and see," said Philip* (John 1:43-46).

When Philip stepped out on his first try at evangelism, Nathanael argued with him concerning Jesus. I have experienced people arguing about Jesus many times and have not always handled it with love and with the right heart. I love the way Philip handled the situation. He took him to Jesus so he could experience this glorious revelation himself.

That is authentic evangelism— connecting people directly to Jesus.

You might not be able to take people to Jesus in person, but you can lead people to Him in many ways, including through the use of the gifts of the Spirit, the laying on of hands, and prayer. Philip did not argue with him one bit. He just brought him to the place where he could connect with Jesus. That is authentic evangelism—connecting people directly to Jesus. The devil tried to lure Philip into an argument, but he did not fall for it. Do not argue with people. Instead, connect people with Jesus.

Philip could have been offended by what Nathanael said—it seemed that Nathanael was mocking him—but he did not take it personally. Even if people mock you, keep your cool and ask God how you can connect that person to Jesus. Philip did not argue, get offended, or take it personally. He just took him to Jesus. Let's begin to develop ways to connect people with Jesus. There is not a one-size-fits-all, cookie-cutter method. All throughout Acts and the Gospels there are many different ways used to connect people with Jesus. Methods ranged from casting out a legion of demons, spitting in mud to heal the blind, having a word of knowledge for a stranger at a well, standing up and proclaiming the Gospel with power, healing a cripple at the gate of the city, and many more. Therefore, we just have to be sensitive to exactly what God is saying in every instance, and this does not happen overnight. We must cultivate and develop through prayer and practice the gifts God has given and will give us.

John continues the narrative, describing the meeting of Jesus and Nathanael:

> When Jesus saw Nathanael approaching, he said of him, "Here truly is an Israelite in whom there is no deceit." "How do you know me?" Nathanael asked. Jesus answered, "I saw you while you were still under the fig tree before Philip called you." Then Nathanael declared, "Rabbi, you are the Son of God; you are the king of Israel." Jesus said, "You believe because I told you I saw you under the fig tree. You will see greater things than that" (John 1:47-50).

When Jesus saw Nathanael, He exhorted him with a word of encouragement. This was such a prophetic word to Nathanael that he asked Jesus how He knew him. Jesus did not bring up the words Nathanael spoke when he said, "Can anything good come out of Nazareth?" Instead, He showed grace. In our evangelism and ministry, we must show love and grace even if there is an undertone of negativity in part of our message (i.e. "all have sinned," "you're a sinner." In fact, we should let them draw that conclusion from the scriptures we share and questions we ask).

Jesus went on to reveal things to Nathanael that required special knowledge. First, He commented on his righteous character, and second He spoke of seeing him under the fig tree. Based on Nathanael's startling response, some commentators have concluded that the fig tree was a place that Nathanael used as a private place of prayer. This revelation solicited from Nathanael his proclamation that Jesus was the Messiah. It also revealed to Nathanael that Jesus had His eye on him first. Now Nathanael was convinced that He was the Messiah. Jesus ministered to him in a very personal way; that is the kindness of God that brings people to Jesus. We must continually ask God to develop this beautiful discernment within us in our day-to-day evangelism.

> We must continually ask God to develop this beautiful discernment within us in our day-to-day evangelism.

Jesus saw the situation as an opportunity to build and encourage Nathanael rather than to bring up what he had said to Philip. Jesus sided with grace rather than rebuke. (At times, a rebuke is necessary to bring men to repentance. The story of Nathan and David is a good example of this [see 2 Sam. 12], but that is the exception rather than the rule.)

Holy Spirit, thank You for the gift of prophecy that You give to Your children. I ask You today for a greater impartation of the prophetic. Thank You for using me to prophesy in the past, but I ask You to use me with divine accuracy and greater dimensions in the future. Use me to prophesy over people who have never gone to church and do not have a relationship with You. Use me at my work, at the store, on the plane, with my neighbors—anywhere and everywhere I can edify and bring people to You.

Chapter 7

THE LIGHTNING OF GOD

Before moving to Texas to serve alongside pastor/evangelist Steve Hill, I was there for a weekend mobilizing the church for an outreach weekend. During the outreach the "college and career" pastor and I were riding around checking on all of the teams that were involved in the outreach. We pulled up to one of the teams and he asked for the team of Trisha and Eli to split up. He sent me with Trisha because I had told him earlier I thought she was very beautiful. (Fortunately for me, she would later become my wife!)

We didn't know one another at all. At the third door we visited, a lady came to the door and as I was introducing ourselves to her she began to shut the door in our faces. Now we were not engaged in confrontational evangelism at the time. We were simply going from house to house letting people know our church cared for them and to see if there was anything we could pray with them about. Well we didn't even have a chance to fully engage this lady before the door began to shut.

As she was shutting the door, I received a word of knowledge and raised my voice and rebuked a spirit of depression off of her life. When I said that, the door that was nearly completely shut, swung wide open. She stepped outside and began to weep. Without asking Trisha if she was okay with the idea or if the lady would be okay with us laying hands on her I just told Trisha all at once to lay hands on her stomach. When she did, I rebuked a spirit of infirmity and proclaimed that she would be healed. She was touched mightily by the power of God.

The next night we held our final meeting where we were going to conclude our weekend. The lady who was touched so powerfully showed up. She wanted to testify to what God had done in her life. She said, "I was severely depressed for three months and hadn't left to go outside of my house during that time. I had also battled a chronic intestinal disease for 30 years and at the moment they took authority, the miracle began." She was so excited that God had not only broken the depression off of her life but healed her as well!

> If there were ever a time for us to pray that God would use us and infuse us with power from on high in a fresh way, that time is today!

The Word of God is filled with individuals, churches, ministers, cities, and entire nations that have been impacted by the Spirit of God. The church of Jesus Christ in America and around the world is in a place where we desperately need a fresh personal, corporate, national, and even a global awakening. In this hour when biblical values are deemed as largely irrelevant, society has drifted to the attitude *whatever feels good, gives you pleasure, or makes you happy, go for it.* We need a jolt from heaven! Throughout God's Word we often find before God moves, He gets hold of an individual and uses them to turn the tide. If there were ever a time for us to pray that God would use us and infuse us with power from on high in a fresh way, that time is today!

Compared to the Gospels and the book of Acts, we have lowered the bar in our walks and in our churches to some new acceptable level. We should never judge our lives based on our fellow neighbor or even godly leaders. It's never wrong to desire and ask God for certain attributes and different anointings that some leaders carry, but that's not the ultimate goal. Our goal as believers and churches should be to bear a reflection of Christ in purity and to demonstrate the power of God as He did. And we should desire to imitate the different men and women in God's Word who demonstrated earth-shaking power. For example, Peter's shadow healed the sick. To my knowledge, my shadow has never healed anyone. That being the case, there is another dimension of power available to me if I can position myself and continually press in to God for this anointing to manifest in my life.

Too often we settle for less than God's best and never contend to walk in true New Testament power as normal for every believer. The bar is far beyond living a clean, holy life before God. The bar is so far from "good" church services and God's presence during worship, which I am not minimizing. Part of the norm in Acts was that everyone who showed up was healed. In our church services today, a healing is hit or miss at best, and it would be celebrated beyond description if everyone who walked into a service was healed in a particular service; it's not the norm. However, that was normal through the ministry of Christ and the apostles in the book of Acts, at least, where faith was not lacking.

Transformed in a Moment of Time

Moses is a great example of someone who ministers before a real encounter with God. Could this be where many of us are today? There are notable times in which Moses moved prior to his encounter. One thing that we are absolutely sure of is that Moses had a burden for the people of God to be free from the bondage of the Egyptians. He was called by God to see the Hebrews set free. But we see that it takes more than the call to fulfill and complete what God has called one to accomplish.

God never told Moses to kill that Egyptian. However, he had an overwhelming burden to see them set free. This act shows us that we should not step out in our own wisdom, ability, and strength. Neither the church nor Christians should function in this pattern. Many have a tremendous call and will to do what God would have them do, but they operate in their own power and there's a void of the supernatural power to fulfill the work. When we are involved in the work of the Lord, we must examine the situation with the view that we will fail if God doesn't sovereignly move. Too often we can accomplish our goals and work without the supernatural.

I love what I heard evangelist Reinhard Bonnke say at a conference several years back. Paraphrasing, he said, "If you take the supernatural out of the Bible you have nothing left but some periods and commas. The Word of God is a supernatural word with a supernatural Jesus." This statement is quite revealing. If you take the supernatural activity out of creation, you don't have creation. If you take the supernatural out of the lives of practically every person in the Bible, they have no ministry at all. Noah would have drowned because he wouldn't have heard God's supernatural voice and instruction. Daniel would have been eaten by a pride of lions were it not for the supernatural activity of angels. Elijah would have been killed by the prophets of Baal before fire would have fallen from heaven. Jonah would have died in the water if it were not for the belly of a whale. Moses would have been killed by Pharaoh if God hadn't shown Himself strong time and time again. Paul wouldn't have been set free from prison if the angels of the Lord hadn't set him free. Peter would have left the lame man sitting on the way to his morning prayer without the supernatural activity of God. Jesus would have sunk trying to walk on the water. Lazarus would still be dead and Jesus would have never been resurrected. Not to mention Samson, Elisha, Esther, Samuel, David, and Jacob—just to scratch the surface. So if you take the supernatural out, what would we have left? The entire foundation of Christianity is built on signs, wonders, and miracles. Where are they today as they were in the days of God's Word? They haven't ceased; we've just been satisfied to live without them.

> The entire foundation of Christianity is built on signs, wonders, and miracles. Where are they today as they were in the days of God's Word? They haven't ceased; we've just been satisfied to live without them.

What would happen if the supernatural were not in operation in your life? Would many things cease? What happened when it wasn't operating in the life of Moses? Utter failure. But thanks be to God, He was faithful to encounter Moses and anoint him with power.

Pre-encounter Moses failed. Post-encounter Moses moved in one of the most powerful ministries in the entire Word of God. If the supernatural were not involved in his life, his ministry would have completely failed and Pharaoh would have killed him. He would have died at the Red Sea and not been able to cross. They would've starved to death, their clothes would've worn out, disease would've wiped them out, they would've been completely lost and at times not had any water at all, just to name a few calamities.

> ## If we take a risk and go, God will show!

We can't overlook the point that Moses put it all on the line. He took a risk. God uses risk-takers. If he had not taken the risk, he would not have witnessed God's power, even post-encounter. Some come to church and receive encounter after encounter and never take a risk. Take a risk and step out the next time you see someone in a wheelchair, blind, dead, or bound by the devil. Nothing times nothing equals nothing. Begin to take risks and you will see God's power. Here is simple pattern that we can see again and again throughout the word: *an ordinary man or woman encounters a divine God, who empowers them from heaven above. They step out, take a risk, and go. Then, and only then, does God move in power. If we take a risk and go, God will show!*

Before Moses's encounter, he failed; post-encounter, he flourished. This gives us a foundation and unabashedly confirms that it is God's plan and desire for every believer to never settle where we are, nor be satisfied with moving in anything less than God's supernatural power.

If you are not moving in power at this point, *do not condemn yourself!* Focus on what God said He would do. Thank Him for what He has done. Continue to believe to move in everything He promises that is available. Never allow your mind to stay in what He hasn't done or seems He is not doing. Always keep the bar set on how Jesus and the great saints of the Word operated and let that be your bar, void of condemnation.

Changing Our Thinking Process

From that time Jesus began to preach, and to say, Repent: for the kingdom of heaven is at hand (Matthew 4:17 KJV).

Jesus's first message instructed everyone to repent. We often think the word *repentance* means merely "to turn from sin," but that is not the Greek definition of the word. It actually means: "to change the way you think." Turning from your sin is a fruit of the word *repent* or *repentance*. This is very telling that this was Jesus's first sermon according to Matthew. Out of everything He could have started with, it was this principle. Jesus was revealing this principle from the get-go: "You have to get ahold of your mind and the way you process thoughts and make them line up with every word that proceeds from My mouth and God's Word so you can move and manifest the Kingdom of God and its power."

I once heard Bill Johnson give this analogy: when you bowl, your initial goal is to correctly line up with the arrows in the lane. That is your place to start, but not your target; the pins are the target. Turning from sin is hitting the arrow, but is, unfortunately, where many people stop. Many repent (change the way they think) enough to get to heaven, but not enough to see the Kingdom of Heaven at hand. The goal Jesus had in mind was twofold: 1) That people would turn from their sin, which is very important and should never be minimized; and 2) That people would change the way they think in order to reveal the Kingdom of Heaven at hand.

Jesus was saying, "The Kingdom's power is ready and available to you right now. If you do not change your religious mindset or turn from your sin, you will never see the Kingdom. Therefore, change the way you think so you can see the Kingdom and its power!" Jesus was trying to get them to take their eyes off the natural and anchor their faith in the unseen. There is still an unseen realm that only God can spiritually reveal to us; we must not rely on what we see with our natural eyes. We cannot always see the Kingdom and its power, but it is very real and present. *"So we fix our eyes not on what is seen, but on what is unseen, since what is seen is temporary, but what is unseen is eternal"* (2 Cor. 4:18).

Let us filter every belief we have through God's Word and experiences that are backed by His Word. Oftentimes, people will build core beliefs off of a failure or something God didn't seem to do. For example, "I've prayed for many people in wheelchairs and have never seen one arise and walk." This experience does not set a principle of what God teaches—in fact, it contradicts God's Word. We must retrain our thought processes that don't line up with scripture, countering all experiences with God's Word. For too long the church has changed its interpretation of scripture to match its experiences (thus cessationism)—time to do just the opposite and expect the principles of scripture to be fleshed out in our experiences.

> For too long the church has changed its interpretation of scripture to match its experiences—time to do just the opposite and expect the principles of scripture to be fleshed out in our experiences.

Are you thinking, "I've never been used to see the lame healed. God must not or will not use me in this area" versus "With man it's impossible, but with God all things are possible" (see Mark 10:27)? Peter and John were at the gate in Acts 3:1, and a lame man was healed in the name of Jesus. Is there still power in the name of Jesus? Do you believe it? Do you really believe it? Jesus said, *"Very truly I tell you, whoever believes in me will do the works I have been doing, and they will do even greater things than these, because I am going to the Father"* (John 14:12). You better believe, because it's a Kingdom principle and the Kingdom is here, right now. It's as true as the principle of salvation. Do you believe you're saved? Then you should believe in the healing power of Christ.

You may think, "I don't really have the personality or charisma to lead someone to Christ." God is telling you: "You can do all things through Christ who gives you strength" (see Phil. 4:13).

You may say, "I'll never be used in the prophetic or other power gifts like so many in God's Word were." God says, "Whatsoever you ask for in prayer by faith you shall receive" (see Matt. 21:22 and Mark 11:24).

As we align our thought processes with God's Word, it sets our feet on a rock to combat the fiery darts of hell. (We will look deeper into using God's Word in the next chapter.) Another help in this process is to have a real manifest encounter with God's power. *Encountering God's power changes everything.*

Encountering God's power
changes everything.

Lightning Strikes—in Apostolic Times *and* Our Times

The apostle Paul is a classic example of God's power to transform and change through supernatural manifestations. When we first encounter him in the scriptures (as Saul, at the stoning of Stephen, Acts 7–8), he is an unapologetic persecutor of the church. He felt it was his mandate from God to martyr believers, until his trip to Damascus one day. In a twinkling of an eye, God showed up in a display of glory and power and Paul was transformed for the rest of his life with this one moment being the catalyst.

He was transformed from persecutor to the persecuted. He changed from unbelief in Christ to laying down his life for Christ. This man was never the same again from the inside out, and he spent the rest of his life declaring, defending, and moving in miraculous power through his ministry and writing vast amounts of the New Testament after this encounter with Christ on the road to Damascus.

One day I was having some coffee in the middle of an extended fast in the coffee section of a bookstore. I was sitting with a friend having a conversation about prayer. The person next to me overheard our conversation, and about that same time I received a prophetic word for this particular lady. I began to prophesy to her and compared her to the life of Hannah and her barrenness. I told her, "As Hannah was barren, you're barren, and God wants to use you to give birth." Never having met this woman in my life, and not knowing her at all, I said this by faith in what I felt God speaking to me.

In the same manner I didn't know her, I didn't know the person she was with either. But she was actually having a counseling session of some sort with her pastor. When I compared her life to Hannah, she looked at him and he smiled. She said, "Is that the same woman in the Bible you were telling me about?" He said, "Yes!" You could feel the presence of God beginning to intensify.

She looked at me and said, "I have just recently been saved and formerly lived a lesbian lifestyle. I am now married to my husband and had a miscarriage last week." Wow! I asked her, her pastor, and my friend to all join hands together right there in the coffee section as many were looking on. I felt the anointing drop like we were at the altar in the middle of a great outpouring. I then dropped the hands of the two on either side and laid hands on her head and said, "Fire!" When I did, the power of God hit her like a freight train. She fell on the hardwood floor in the coffee section of the bookstore. It was wild. Her pastor tried to hold her up with all his might, but she was out cold and as limp as a corpse. She was laid out right on the floor.

People began to look at us awfully funny. I didn't know the exact protocol for this kind of manifestation in public with so many unbelievers and religious people looking at us. One guy full of religion came right up to her and looked down with this grim stare. So I just shouted out to everybody, "Can I have everyone's attention please? This woman hasn't had a heart attack or anything like that at all. She has been hit by the fire of the Holy Spirit and will be just fine."

I'd like to say many wanted to receive prayer, but that's not what happened at all. The manager came over to me and said they were going to call the authorities and an ambulance. I completely understood why she would have to do that, especially not trusting it was a move of God happening in the middle of her store. About that time, the lady got up off of the floor and said something like this: "I was depressed and now I'm set free. Leave him alone!" Now you have to understand, she was out on the floor for around four to five minutes. You may say that's not very long if that's happened to you at church for even longer. But this wasn't a church. Go lie down on the floor at your nearest coffee shop without moving one muscle and you will see that five minutes can seem like an eternity.

After she got up, she said to me, "I could not move one muscle, but I could hear everything that was being said." She went on to say, "I didn't believe in the power of God like that, but I do now!" It was unbelievable! God desires and is willing to take over any situation anywhere if we allow Him to move through us.

A side note to this story is that I had been praying specifically for God to open a door for me to preach. I was home itinerating as a missionary and needed opportunities to share in churches what I was doing. That pastor invited me to come and preach. God is ready to work with us; we just have to be willing to take that step.

One Manifestation from God Turned the City Upside Down

They sailed to the region of the Gerasenes, which is across the lake from Galilee. When Jesus stepped ashore, he was met by a demon-possessed man from the town. For a long time this man had not worn clothes or lived in a house, but had lived in the tombs. When he saw Jesus, he cried out and fell at his feet, shouting at the top of his voice, "What do you want with me, Jesus, Son of the Most High God? I beg you, don't torture me!" For Jesus had commanded the impure spirit to come out of the man (Luke 8:26-29).

As soon as Jesus stepped into the boat to sail over, the collision began (see Luke 8:22–25). Jesus spoke out loud, "Let's go over to the other side of the lake." When He said this, the demons who had control over this region heard Jesus's words and attacked Him on the way. A great storm came upon the boat and seasoned fishermen were afraid for their lives. Seasoned fishermen would not set sail into a dangerous storm. The enemy waited until they were on their way so that he could attack them at their most vulnerable point. The devil knew that if Jesus got His foot on the shore it was all over. However, the devil did not have control over the area without a conduit—that is, the demon-possessed man.

Thus, this was not a human battle; it was a battle between kingdoms. Ephesians 6:12 says, *"For our struggle is not against flesh and blood, but against the rulers, against the authorities, against the powers of this dark world and against the spiritual forces of evil in the heavenly realms."* This was a classic showdown of two kingdoms colliding.

A key point of the enemy's attack while they were at sea was to test the seriousness of the men. He will not mess with you very much as you sit happily in church, but when you step out and get in the boat to do battle, he will come. We are backed with the most powerful Kingdom in the universe. Jesus said many times, "Fear not." When Jesus got in the boat and the storm came, He was not afraid because He knew what Kingdom He represented. When you are on a Kingdom mission you have Kingdom power, even over nature, to get the job done.

> The enemy will not mess with you very much as you sit happily in church, but when you step out and get in the boat to do battle, he will come.

The Bible tells us that this demon-possessed man had been bound by the devil for a long time. The devil had that whole area in turmoil for some time. This man was so possessed that he even lost sense of his natural needs. Two basic necessities of life are clothes and a place to sleep in peace. The devil stole both of these from him. He lived naked in tombs among the dead. Demonic torture in this man's life was severe and had been occurring for many years.

When they reached the land, Jesus did not have to find him or make one thing happen. This man who had kept this countryside in turmoil came running and bowed down to Jesus. He began to plead with Him not to torture him. That is a quick victory! Jesus came in the power of the Kingdom of God. Matthew 12:28 says, *"But if it is by the Spirit of God that I drive out demons, then the kingdom of God has come upon you."* There is no struggle when the Kingdom manifests in power because there is no other power that can come close to the power and authority of the Kingdom of God.

> There is no struggle when the Kingdom manifests in power because there is no other power that can come close to the power and authority of the Kingdom of God.

For Jesus had commanded the impure spirit to come out of the man. Many times it had seized him, and though he was chained hand and foot and kept under guard, he had broken his chains and had been driven by the demon into solitary places. Jesus asked him, "What is your name?" "Legion," he replied, because many demons had gone into him. And they begged Jesus repeatedly not to order them to go into the Abyss. A large herd of pigs was feeding there on the hillside. The demons begged Jesus to let them go into the pigs, and he gave them permission. When the demons came out of the man, they went into the pigs, and the herd rushed down the steep bank into the lake and was drowned. When those tending the pigs saw what had happened, they ran off and reported this in the town and countryside, and the people went out to see what had happened. When they came to Jesus, they found the man from whom the demons had gone out, sitting at Jesus' feet, dressed and in his right mind; and they were afraid. Those who had seen it told the people how the demon-possessed man had been cured. Then all the people of the region of the Gerasenes asked Jesus to leave them, because they were overcome with fear. So he got into the boat and left. The man from whom the demons had gone out begged to go with him, but Jesus sent him away, saying, "Return home and tell how much God has done for you." So the man went away and told all over town how much Jesus had done for him (Luke 8:29-39).

Jesus commanded the demons to come out with one sentence. All the years of bondage the man had suffered came to an end when Jesus spoke. *There wasn't a struggle at all.* God wants to use His people to speak the Word and see His Kingdom established in an entire region. When the two kingdoms collided, God's Kingdom did not only win, it dominated.

When the two kingdoms collided, God's Kingdom did not only win, it dominated.

The whole region of people there heard what had happened. This man, who had kept the area in turmoil year after year, was now made whole in just a matter of minutes! This was not a twelve-step program or a five-day deliverance session; it was one step with the King. We have the authority to walk in the one-step program. When Jesus ministered to a person, they left healed, delivered, and set free with one step. We can do it, as well.

Lord, thank You for what You did through Moses, David, Peter, and Paul! But God, I pray that You use me! Thank You for what You have done through my life, but I'm not satisfied with where I am. I ask You to empower me with a greater anointing of signs and wonders to draw more people who do not know You than ever before. I can do nothing without Your empowerment. I humble myself before You, knowing my greatest efforts in the flesh do not compare to Your power. In Jesus's name, amen.

Chapter 8

STANDING ON
GOD'S WORD

One night in Dallas, Texas, at a popular gay and lesbian district, we were doing our Friday night outreach. This particular outreach consisted of worship, sharing God's love and grace, and getting to know the regulars so that we might win many to Christ. I wouldn't say the majority, but some of them hated us being down there worshiping. They would call the cops on us and make up stories to try and get us run off. Someone called the police this particular night.

We could have been singing about Buddha, Muhammad, or just singing some rock-n-roll song and no one would have ever bothered us, but because we were singing about Jesus, it shook the atmosphere. We weren't yelling at people, cornering them, or being aggressive in any way. We were just simply worshiping Jesus with a few acoustic instruments. With that being said, they sent six patrol cars and many officers. You would have thought we were causing a riot. When I saw the police, I felt God give me a scripture from Exodus where Moses was told by God that He would drive back the opposition and set their borders.

> *See, I am sending an angel ahead of you to guard you along the way and to bring you to the place I have prepared. Pay attention to him and listen to what he says. Do not rebel against him; he will not forgive your rebellion, since my Name is in him. If you listen carefully to what he says and do all that I say, I will be an enemy to your enemies and will oppose those who oppose you. My angel will go ahead of you and bring you into the land of the Amorites, Hittites, Perizzites, Canaanites, Hivites and Jebusites, and I will wipe them out* (Exodus 23:20-23).

Our battle was not against police officers by any stretch of the imagination. Nor was it against the people who didn't want us singing about Jesus. It was against evil spirits and principalities that are at work through people.

Our battle was not against police officers by any stretch of the imagination. Nor was it against the people who didn't want us singing about Jesus. It was against evil spirits and principalities that are at work through people. *"For our struggle is not against flesh and blood, but against the rulers, against the authorities, against the powers of this dark world and against the spiritual forces of evil in the heavenly realms"* (Eph. 6:12). There were around 40 to 50 Bible school students I was leading this particular night. (I've even had times when the Lord intervened when authorities told us to leave. They would change their minds and let us stay.) I knew God could give us favor, but I wanted the team to experience it as well so that they could take this experience with them in their ministry.

We began to read aloud this passage and agree with it through prayer. There are times when you can say nice quiet prayers, but there are others when you should be much more aggressive. *"From the days of John the Baptist until now the kingdom of heaven suffers violence, and the violent take it by force"* (Matt. 11:12 NKJV). This passage refers to spiritually taking it by force because the police were not our enemy; we are called to respect authority. But we can wage war against the spiritual darkness. So I had the team lift their voices and agree with this passage in prayer. We cried out with a loud voice that God would send His angel to war against powers of darkness and that He would push them back. We were asking God to give us favor with the police as well. We began to read further in the passage and agreed with it, too.

> *I will make all your enemies turn their backs and run. I will send the hornet ahead of you to drive the Hivites, Canaanites and Hittites out of your way. But I will not drive them out in a single year, because the land would become desolate and the wild animals too numerous for you. Little by little I will drive them out before you, until you have increased enough to take possession of the land. I will establish your borders from the Red Sea to the Mediterranean Sea,*

and from the desert to the Euphrates River (Exodus 23:27-31).

As we prayed this *now word* from God, we were very specific. We were standing on a small concrete peninsula that was off the sidewalk and divided parking, yet was butted up to the street. So we cried out to God, "Give us this 10-by-10 area as our border! We are not enough in number to take the whole area, so give us this 10-by-10 area. You are a boundary-setting God and You control the boundaries and nobody else. God, grant us favor and establish it through the police. Have them say, 'This is your area.' Give us possession of the land." We also prayed Luke 4:18, *"The Spirit of the Lord is on me, because he has anointed me to proclaim good news to the poor. He has sent me to proclaim freedom for the prisoners and recovery of sight for the blind, to set the oppressed free."* "God, as You grant us this 10-by-10 area, we ask You to make this a plot of ground where the captives are set free. Let it be so mighty, God, that all who are oppressed by the devil on this ground be set free. God, we pray that people will be hit by the power of God right here this week and the weeks to come!"

Around that time, we were tenaciously going after God with our voices lifted high and everyone seeing it (including the police officers), and the police began to approach us. I stopped praying and politely went over to submit to the officer. I told him what we were doing and he said something like this, "Well, I guess you can stay on this small plot and nowhere else." God had given us the victory!

The next Friday we were back! With the last victory, we were believing for the manifestation of our Luke 4:18 prayer. We prayed Luke 4 again. That night there were two gay men hit so powerfully by the power of God that they fell to the ground. One of them was the brother of an individual who worked with a church I have ministered at. When he left, he called his brother and told him how powerful it was and how God was moving in his life and revealing Himself to him. He came back and wanted prayer again. When I followed up with him, he told me that God visited him again the next day. As we took authority and dominion over the area, God broke in with great power. To my knowledge, that team we birthed still meets most Friday nights on that same plot reaching that area with the love of Christ.

Before we delve into operating according to God's Word, let's take a look at how the devil will distort God's Word to deceive us if we are not fully grounded. This has been one of his main strategies since the Garden of Eden. The enemy is deceitful at his core, and when he speaks he lies. I love the way John describes him:

> *He was a murderer from the beginning, not holding to the truth, for there is no truth in him. When he lies, he speaks his native language, for he is a liar and the father of lies* (John 8:44).

Often, he will not outright oppose God's Word; he will just twist it a bit in hopes that we fall into his trap and are swept totally off course. Let's take a look at his first deception and how he perverted God's Word:

> *The Lord God took the man and put him in the Garden of Eden to work it and take care of it. And the Lord God commanded the man, "You are free to eat from any tree in the garden; but you must not eat from the tree of the knowledge of good and evil, for when you eat from it you will certainly die"* (Genesis 2:15-17).

Now the serpent was more crafty than any of the wild animals the Lord God had made. He said to the woman, "Did God really say, 'You must not eat from any tree in the garden'?" The woman said to the serpent, "We may eat fruit from the trees in the garden, but God did say, 'You must not eat fruit from the tree that is in the middle of the garden, and you must not touch it, or you will die.'" "You will not certainly die," the serpent said to the woman. "For God knows that when you eat from it your eyes will be opened, and you will be like God, knowing good and evil." When the woman saw that the fruit of the tree was good for food and pleasing to the eye, and also desirable for gaining wisdom, she took some and ate it. She also gave some to her husband, who was with her, and he ate it. Then the eyes of both of them were opened, and they realized they were naked; so they sewed fig leaves together and made coverings for themselves (Genesis 3:1-7).

The devil loves to put a question in the mind of man concerning what God said. If he can get you to question God's Word, he has you started down the road to full-blown deception. Eve's first response to the devil was excellent. She quoted God's Word directly, "We may eat fruit from the trees in the garden, but God did say, 'You must not eat fruit from the tree that is in the middle of the garden, and you must not touch it, or you will die.'"

Then the devil responded with a lie. (A good way to discern when the devil is lying is that his lips are moving—*when he lies, he speaks his native language*.) "You will not certainly die," the serpent said to the woman. "For God knows that when you eat from it your eyes will be opened, and you will be like God, knowing good and evil." At that very moment, instead of standing on what God said, she began to question God's Word. As she began to process this, she was tempted.

> *But each person is tempted when they are dragged away by their own evil desire and enticed. Then, after desire has conceived, it gives birth to sin; and sin, when it is full-grown, gives birth to death* (James 1:14-15).

Never allow our hearts to be deceived by the subtle twist of God's Word.

Her temptation began to drag her away. "It looks sooooo good and God really won't mind. I'll just do it this one time." In one moment of time she and Adam fell from the position they had. They must have regretted it for the rest of their lives. They learned a tough lesson and it's one we always need to keep in front of us. Never allow our hearts to be deceived by the subtle twist of God's Word.

We see the same effort pointed squarely at Jesus, the Son of God. The devil didn't change his game plan that had ravaged millions. He went straight for the tactic of distorting God's Word. He must have thought, "I've got to hit Him with my best shot." So he went for deception. Let's look at the conversation.

> *The devil said to him, "If you are the Son of God, tell this stone to become bread." Jesus answered, "It is written: 'Man shall not live on bread alone.'" The*

devil led him up to a high place and showed him in an instant all the kingdoms of the world. And he said to him, "I will give you all their authority and splendor; it has been given to me, and I can give it to anyone I want to. If you worship me, it will all be yours." Jesus answered, "It is written: 'Worship the Lord your God and serve him only.'" The devil led him to Jerusalem and had him stand on the highest point of the temple. "If you are the Son of God," he said, "throw yourself down from here. For it is written: 'He will command his angels concerning you to guard you carefully; they will lift you up in their hands, so that you will not strike your foot against a stone.'" Jesus answered, "It is said: 'Do not put the Lord your God to the test.'" When the devil had finished all this tempting, he left him until an opportune time (Luke 4:3-13).

Jesus didn't get into an open-ended conversation with the devil. He quoted God's Word and didn't back off. He didn't begin to question and ponder things, but let God's Word speak for itself and stood in that position.

Jesus didn't get into an open-ended conversation with the devil. He quoted God's Word and didn't back off. He didn't begin to question and ponder things, but let God's Word speak for itself and stood in that position. If the devil can get you to question what God said, he's in the process of moving you. It may not even be him leading you into sin but simply causing you to question God's call upon your life or something God has spoken to you. You may not be seeing everything come to pass and not realize that you're at the brink of your destiny. The devil will try his best to discourage you to back off the call. Don't listen to it! If God has called you, don't question it or allow your mind to get diverted. Set your mind and affection on what He said and never ever back off! The devil will say that your child will not get saved, but the scripture says your household shall be saved! He might try and tell you that you'll die with that sickness. Rather than believe that, believe by His stripes you are healed. The enemy tried to use someone close to Christ to divert Him from His destiny. Let's see how He responded.

> *From that time on Jesus began to explain to his disciples that he must go to Jerusalem and suffer many things at the hands of the elders, the chief priests and the teachers of the law, and that he must be killed and on the third day be raised to life. Peter took him aside and began to rebuke him. "Never, Lord!" he said. "This shall never happen to you!" Jesus turned and said to Peter, "Get behind me, Satan! You are a stumbling block to me; you do not have in mind the concerns of God, but merely human concerns"* (Matthew 16:21-23).

This is a stark contrast to what He just said to Peter literally one moment earlier. "Upon this rock I will build My church." Jesus made this statement because Peter had just stated that Jesus was the Messiah. With Peter's next statement, he says something preposterous. It definitely didn't line up with God's Word for His Son. This shows us that we are flesh with clay feet and we don't always get it right. This is why it's paramount to not be dictated by emotions but allow God's Word to guide us. The devil was using a godly man to distort the Word. It's probable that people close to you may try and divert you from God's specific word and plan for your life at various times.

> When someone or something comes against what God has called us to do or His perfect plan for us, we must aggressively assault it and leave no room for any question on where we stand.

Jesus didn't deal passively with Peter's misstatement; He aggressively rebuked him and put him in his place. When someone or something comes against what God has called us to do or His perfect plan for us, we must aggressively assault it and leave no room for any question on where we stand. The enemy used David's brothers to try and divert him from what God called him to do, but he aggressively refuted them. That is just one of many examples. As Jesus completely obliterated distractions, let us follow His example and do the same when something or someone attacks the call of God on our life.

The apostles were told by religious leaders that they could preach whatever they chose, as long as they took out the name of Jesus. It would have been much easier on them if they had taken out that one piece. Let's take a closer look at what would happen if we removed that one name. First off, Jesus really isn't one little piece. If you took out the name Jesus, you wouldn't have a cross. There would not have been miracle ministry. There wouldn't be a perfect lamb to erase sin. The glorious resurrection would have been eradicated. They were radically opposed to removing just *one* word. Needless to say, everything else would have been taken out of the message without Jesus. Don't back off one word or one principle God has given you to do or speak. Taking out or removing one aspect of your call could alter the whole destiny of what God has called you to do. If it's preaching salvation, preach salvation. Don't start preaching something else, but stick with your message. It's not about what's popular or if someone told you to back off words like the cross, the blood, sin, and holiness. *Imagine how many souls could be lost for eternity if you divert.* Take nothing away and stay true to your assignment. Let the apostles be your example—cling with all your might to your calling and your assignment.

> Don't back off one word or one principle God has given you to do or speak. Taking out or removing one aspect of your call could alter the whole destiny of what God has called you to do.

For me personally, a part of my call is to address sin. Sometimes it's not popular, but it's definitely necessary. We should never judge other people's callings. Some are called to teach. Some God has given a message of encouragement to the body of Christ. Others are focused on healing. This is why it's so important that we honor one another's call. It is also important that if you lean toward one strength, you should bring others in and around you who have different strengths than yourself, even if you're uncomfortable. This is how the body is built up according to Ephesians 4.

Drawing the Sword of Authority

Let's take a look at a powerful process and discipline we can live by to withstand the fiery darts of hell and advance the Kingdom of God. A major key is to stay grounded in simple truths from the Word of God. One of those truths is a clear principle that I try to live by: *You can have what the Bible says you can have.* But first, remember that when we read the Bible we must apply it to our lives by *faith*, for *"without faith it is impossible to please God"* (Heb. 11:6). It is imperative that we believe God's Word above every doubt and challenge we face. The believer's authority begins and ends with God's Word.

> You can have what the Bible
> says you can have.

In order to fully walk in all that God has for us and to use the authority He has given us, we must have a renewed mind. Romans 12:2 says, *"Do not conform to the pattern of this world, but be transformed by the renewing of your mind. Then you will be able to test and approve what God's will is—his good, pleasing and perfect will."* We renew our minds through the Word of God and not simply through our own thoughts. When we have a thought that does not line up with God's Word, we must cast it down. Second Corinthians 10:4-5 says, *"The weapons we fight with are not the weapons of the world. On the contrary, they have divine power to demolish strongholds. We demolish arguments and every pretension that sets itself up against the knowledge of God, and we take captive every thought to make it obedient to Christ."* The Word of God should be the filter of our mind and any thought that is contrary to the Word should be discarded.

The following creation passage from Genesis speaks point-edly of our authority:

> *Then God said, "Let us make mankind in our image, in our likeness, so that they may rule over the fish in the sea and the birds in the sky, over the livestock and all the wild animals, and over all the creatures that move along the ground." So God created mankind in his own image, in the image of God he created them; male and female he created them. God blessed them and said to them, "Be fruitful and increase in number; fill the earth and subdue it. Rule over the fish in the sea and the birds in the sky and over every living creature that moves on the ground." Then God said, "I give you every seed-bearing plant on the face of the whole earth and every tree that has fruit with seed in it. They will be yours for food. And to all the beasts of the earth and all the birds in the sky and all the creatures that move along the ground—everything that has the breath of life in it—I give every green plant for food." And it was so* (Genesis 1:26-30).

God gave us dominion right from the start. Let's look at one of the first statements God made concerning mankind. He said, "Let us make mankind in our image and in our likeness." All throughout the Bible, when God or Jesus spoke, something happened. Part of what the image and likeness God gave us was the power to speak things into proper alignment. When God said "Let there be light," there was light. When Jesus spoke to Lazarus to come forth while he was dead and in the tomb, he came forth. At the very words of Christ, Lazarus was raised from the dead.

The Roman centurion understood well this principle of authority:

> When Jesus had entered Capernaum, a centurion came to him, asking for help. "Lord," he said, "my servant lies at home paralyzed, suffering terribly." Jesus said to him, "Shall I come and heal him?" The centurion replied, "Lord, I do not deserve to have you come under my roof. But just say the word, and my servant will be healed. For I myself am a man under authority, with soldiers under me. I tell this one, 'Go,' and he goes; and that one, 'Come,' and he comes. I say to my servant, 'Do this,' and he does it." When Jesus heard this, he was amazed and said to those following him, "Truly I tell you, I have not found anyone in Israel with such great faith." ...Then Jesus said to the centurion, "Go! Let it be done just as you believed it would." And his servant was healed at that moment (Matthew 8:5-10,13).

The story of the centurion is a great example for us today. We see in this passage that faith is the key to walking in authority.

This man had faith that whatever Jesus said would happen, would indeed come to pass. Faith is the link to God's power. It is by faith that we operate in the power of God. Faith accompanied by action releases God's authority in our lives to the world around us and to our circumstances. James tells us that faith must be accompanied by action (see James 2:14–26). James is clear that without works our faith is dead. This man's faith and the words of Jesus produced a miracle.

Jesus is not walking on earth today as He did during the days of the centurion, but we still have His Word. We can unlock the power of His Word through faith. This is a powerful foundation when it comes to evangelism. We must do more than just believe that the promises of Jesus are for us; we must also walk them out.

> We must do more than just believe that the promises of Jesus are for us; we must also walk them out.

Let's put these three principles together: 1) We have power to speak the Word of God with the same power that Jesus did because we were created in His image and He told us that we would do greater works than He did (see John 14:12); 2) We must operate through faith that we can have all God says we can have; and 3) We must put these two principles together and take action because without action our faith is dead.

This is key to our evangelism. Many people say they have the greatest message the world has ever known, but they never share it with others. *This does not make sense.* If one really believes they have the greatest message on earth, they would take action.

Taking the message and sharing it with others will release God's authority through our lives as we speak the Word of God.

The very day I wrote this section I had an opportunity to put these principles in action. It was not as dramatic as the previous story but one I believe will encourage you and build your faith. I was sitting in Denny's and received a simple word of knowledge for my waitress. Simply put, a word of knowledge is a gift of the Spirit found in First Corinthians 12 that gives you knowledge about a person or situation that you would not know unless God spoke to you. I felt God speaking to me that she had a financial need in her life and that I needed to leave her a large tip. We signaled her to come back to our table one more time before we left, and I asked her if there was a financial need in her life. She said there was and began to weep right in the middle of the restaurant. I told her that God sees her situation and has not forgotten about her. It touched her deeply because she was having trouble getting her son Christmas presents and was living with her parents. I did not break down the Gospel message, but I planted a seed and she will never forget that God loves her and cares for her every need. However, I plan to follow up with her and I did give her my personal tract.

Again, this is faith in action that reaches the lost—speaking out God's Word to those who are hurting with the belief that God will back you with His Word and His power. This is taking dominion little by little over daily situations that come our way. We should never stop using our God-given dominion. The sharing of our faith should come with a demonstration of power, such as healings or exorcisms. We will look at these aspects of power later.

Not only does Genesis 1 tell us that we were created in the image of God, but it charges us twice to rule the earth and calls for us to subdue it as well. Those are strong words that we have been given. We have to exercise this in many areas of our lives. Not only in preaching the Gospel, but in demonstrating the power of God and taking authority over the enemy. Jesus always took control and authority over the adversary.

> *When they came to the crowd, a man approached Jesus and knelt before him. "Lord, have mercy on my son," he said. "He has seizures and is suffering greatly. He often falls into the fire or into the water. I brought him to your disciples, but they could not heal him." "You unbelieving and perverse generation," Jesus replied, "how long shall I stay with you? How long shall I put up with you? Bring the boy here to me." Jesus rebuked the demon, and it came out of the boy, and he was healed at that moment. Then the disciples came to Jesus in private and asked, "Why couldn't we drive it out?" He replied, "Because you have so little faith. Truly I tell you, if you have faith as small as a mustard seed, you can say to this mountain, 'Move from here to there,' and it will move. Nothing will be impossible for you"* (Matthew 17:14-20).

In this situation Jesus took dominion over the demon and cast it out by His words. His words had great authority over the devil. He did not stand and pray over him and beg God to heal him; He moved in His authority and the boy was instantly healed. We must take authority over sickness and the devil in our daily walk.

Many believers in a similar situation may begin to pray. Not Jesus. He knew the praying must come in advance (see Mark 9:29). He just spoke because He understood the authority that He walked in and possessed. It was an operation of His faith and command together. God gave us Jesus to be our example and desires for us to use our authority as well. According to Matthew, Jesus told the disciples the reason they could not cast out the demon and see the boy get well was not because they didn't have any faith but "because you have so little faith." Jesus worked with them where they were, and later, as we see in the book of Acts, they moved in greater faith. They walked in what Jesus said they could walk in, and everywhere they went the sick were healed and demons were cast out. This should give us hope that our faith can grow.

> Do not focus on what it seems God has not done, but focus on what He said He would do or has done.

I defy doubt and unbelief and try to live my life by this simple concept: *Do not focus on what it seems God has not done, but focus on what He said He would do or has done.* Any time we begin to focus on what it seems He has not done, we allow the enemy to distort our faith. A great example of this comes from a simple teaching I heard on John the Baptist from Bill Johnson.

While in a jail cell toward the end of his life, John sent his disciples to ask Jesus if He was the Messiah or should he expect another (see Matt. 11:2–19). Jesus did not respond with a rebuke but told them to go and report what was taking place and how

God was moving through the miraculous. The miracles included the blind seeing, the lame walking, lepers being cleansed, the deaf hearing, and the dead being raised. Jesus was not merely verifying that He was the Messiah by the miracles He performed; He was trying to focus John's attention on what He was doing and could do.

> Never build a belief or doctrine around what it seems God is not doing, but on what the Word of God says, what God has done, and what He is doing.

Anytime we begin to focus on what it seems God is not doing in our lives, we begin to feed from the table of the enemy of unbelief. Eating from this table long enough will cause you to lose your focus. If John the Baptist could lose his, anyone can. Jesus was encouraging him to shift his focus back in the right place. John had focused on the negative so long that he built a belief system around what God was not doing. He began to question his whole ministry and beliefs. Never build a belief or doctrine around what it seems God is not doing, but on what the Word of God says, what God has done, and what He is doing. If it does not line up with the Bible, we have to filter it out. If we don't, we could fall prey to the same trap as John. We are not above falling into this same trap, so we must set our mind on what God can do and has done. When we focus on the other, the devil will slowly steal our rule and authority. If the enemy can't get you to fall into sin, he will use any tactic he can to deceive you in any way possible.

Does God Have Pets?

God is not a respecter of a certain person. There is nothing in the Word that tells us God only has an elect few who will walk in dominion and have power over the enemy. Many times, what will happen is that an individual will step out to exercise spiritual authority and not see the results he was looking for and let that discourage him. We should never make an excuse or build a doctrine around what did not happen but continually walk in faith for what can happen.

I briefly mentioned ambassadors in an earlier chapter. The Bible calls us *ambassadors*. Second Corinthians 5:20 says, *"We are therefore Christ's ambassadors, as though God were making his appeal through us. We implore you on Christ's behalf: Be reconciled to God."* The definition of the word *ambassador* is *a diplomatic official of the highest rank; sent by one sovereign or state to another as a resident representative.* That is what you are. However, we represent a much higher King and Kingdom than any on earth. We represent the King of kings and serve in a Kingdom that is above all kingdoms.

If the president of the United States sent one of our ambassadors to another nation with a mission or decree, they would have the full support and authority of the United States. He or she would have all the resources America could offer, which includes finances, military, and whatever one would need to fulfill the mission's objective. The ambassador does not go in his or her own authority, but the authority given him by the nation he represents.

We represent the Kingdom of Heaven and Jesus Christ the supreme King. We have His power, resources, and strength backing us. It's time to begin to exercise this ambassadorial position over the enemy and push back the gates of hell. The hour has come to stand and fight from what we have been given and never settle for less. Jesus is worthy and it's our time to set up His Kingdom's embassy throughout the world.

> The devil loves it when Christians do not exercise their authority. The devil is not moved because of who you are but because of who you are in Christ and whom you represent.

The devil loves it when Christians do not exercise their authority. It makes his job much easier. The devil is not moved because of who you are but because of who you are in Christ and whom you represent, as Paul illustrates in this passage:

> *I pray that the eyes of your heart may be enlightened in order that you may know the hope to which he has called you, the riches of his glorious inheritance in his holy people, and his incomparably great power for us who believe. That power is the same as the mighty strength he exerted when he raised Christ from the dead and seated him at his right hand in the heavenly realms, far above all rule and authority, power and dominion, and every name that is invoked, not only in the present age but also in the one to come. And God placed all things under his feet and appointed him to be head over everything*

for the church, which is his body, the fullness of him who fills everything in every way (Ephesians 1:18-23).

And God raised us up with Christ and seated us with him in the heavenly realms in Christ Jesus (Ephesians 2:6).

Now we are seated with Christ in heavenly realms. The power of God that raised Jesus from the dead is living in us. God placed Jesus far above all rule and authority. That means we have rule, dominion, and authority in Christ Jesus. If we have been placed with Christ far above, that means the devil is far below. It is now time to take these promises and walk in them.

Taking Back Our Dominion

God's Word is very clear concerning our position, authority, and the way God sees us. So many times, believers contradict what God said concerning this powerful truth. Many act like the tail and not the head. That completely contradicts what God has said about us and how He sees us. We're the head and not the tail. We're the top and not the bottom. Many believers walk around like they're on the bottom and not the top. For us to take our God-given place and authority, we have to agree and walk in what God says about us and not society. Let's start acting like we're the head and not the tail and on top and not the bottom!

The Lord will make you the head, not the tail. If you pay attention to the commands of the Lord your God that I give you this day and carefully follow them, you will always be at the top, never at the bottom (Deuteronomy 28:13).

That outreach night in Dallas, Texas, we were doing more than just praying scripture. We were praying the scripture that God was saying to us at that very moment. Not something that He had spoken to us three months prior. Many are good at hearing God and standing on what He said, but will often camp out in that same spot and word while God is trying to speak something new. We must agree with what God has said and what God is saying. Everything that God says is backed by His Word and will in no shape, form, or fashion contradict anything in His written Word. Let's look at how Elijah didn't live in what God *had* said, but always lived in what God *was saying*.

> *Then the word of the Lord came to Elijah: "Leave here, turn eastward and hide in the Kerith Ravine, east of the Jordan. You will drink from the brook, and I have directed the ravens to supply you with food there." So he did what the Lord had told him. He went to the Kerith Ravine, east of the Jordan, and stayed there. The ravens brought him bread and meat in the morning and bread and meat in the evening, and he drank from the brook. Some time later the brook dried up because there had been no rain in the land. Then the word of the Lord came to him: "Go at once to Zarephath in the region of Sidon and stay there. I have directed a widow there to supply you with food." So he went to Zarephath* (1 Kings 17:2-10).

God was very clear with Elijah about what to do and where to go. The nation was in a severe drought and he was going to camp out at a particular brook. As he did what God was saying, he was supernaturally provided for. He was fed and water was provided in the exact location God told him to go.

What would have happened if he had stopped praying and let his relationship with God lack a bit? Could God have spoken something fresh, but Elijah would have been stuck in what God *had* said and not what He *was saying*? When the brook dried up, had Elijah been determined to stay where the provision once was, this very well could have been the scenario and Elijah's response: "Lord, You sent me to this brook, and in the name of Yahweh I command the brook to produce water and the ravens to return." He could have done this with great faith, but the ravens would not have come and the brook would have stayed dry because God had given him another address that was going to provide all the provision that he would need.

Many movements and good Christians pray certain scriptures that God isn't saying at that particular moment and get frustrated. Ask God what particular scripture He wants you to pray for in each changing season. Especially if you seem to be hitting a wall in what you know God has said. Ask Him if He is saying something else and pray and agree with that. This was a key to all of Elijah's success. He didn't get stuck in what God had said; his ear was always open to what God was saying.

There are many scriptures we could have prayed that night in Dallas, but God was saying Exodus 23. As we partner and agree with what God is saying, we will see our spiritual authority and dominion strengthen because we are walking in partnership and not flying solo. As we partner with Christ and move in what He is saying, we will see "His Kingdom come and His will be done on earth as it is in heaven."

Lord, we thank You that heaven and earth will pass away, but Your Word never will. God, help me to stand on Your Word when I cannot see any evidence that what I'm believing for is coming to pass. Help me to stand on Your Word in the face of opposition and resistance. Give me grace to continue to believe You will do everything You have said, even when my emotions, feelings, and senses are not there. I decree I will believe no matter what I feel or sense, in Jesus's name.

Chapter 9

THE POWER OF PROCLAMATION

One evening after a time of ministry at a local church, the youth pastor and I went to a local sandwich shop to grab a bite to eat and have some fellowship. As we were picking up our order, we were waited on by a young Buddhist lady. She was 20 years of age and had just moved to America two months earlier. As we were paying for our meal, I asked the young lady a simple question, "Have you ever felt the power of God?" She replied, "No." I then asked, "Would you like to?" and she said, "Yes!" I then gently placed my right hand on her shoulder and prayed that the fire of heaven would touch her life.

We grabbed our sandwiches and headed for the door. I was literally about to put my hand on the door when she began to yell at me, "There's something on me!" Before I could even turn around, she yelled it again, "There's something on me and I don't know what it is!" I turned around looked right at her and said, "It's Jesus."

> *Therefore God exalted him to the highest place and gave him the name that is above every name, that at the name of Jesus every knee should bow, in heaven and on earth and under the earth, and every tongue acknowledge that Jesus Christ is Lord, to the glory of God the Father* (Philippians 2:9-11).

After I said the name *Jesus,* she doubled over under the power of God and began to manifest. She was literally bent over shaking and weeping with such intensity it looked as if she were hyperventilating. She went from calm, composed, and having it all together to undone under the anointing and power of Jesus Christ, all from one second to the next. God actually invaded the restaurant in power! The restaurant was open for business. God didn't care who saw it or who was present. He's just looking for a vessel to move through, anytime or anywhere.

It was a Subway sandwich shop, so if you've ever been in one you know that they are set up in such a manner that there is a counter between the customers and employees. I said, "I'm coming behind the counter!" The other employee was freaking out and said, "You're not allowed; we have the money back here!" I didn't care what he said at that point, I was going to minister deliverance to this dear lady. Needless to say, I got behind the counter. I laid hands on her and she manifested and was delivered of demons. We took her idol relic off and she gave her life to Jesus and denounced Buddha. It was powerful! Now, this just doesn't happen. I was a missionary in a Buddhist nation for over one year. In her 20 years of life, it was nothing but Buddha, and with one touch from heaven, she completely shifted her life and committed to following Jesus.

And so it was with me, brothers and sisters. When I came to you, I did not come with eloquence or human wisdom as I proclaimed to you the testimony about God. For I resolved to know nothing while I was with you except Jesus Christ and him crucified. I came to you in weakness with great fear and trembling. My message and my preaching were not with wise and persuasive words, but with a demonstration of the Spirit's power, so that your faith might not rest on human wisdom, but on God's power (1 Corinthians 2:1-5).

"Where are the deliverers?"

A few months later while driving home after a weekend of ministry, I received a phone call from Wong Chee; this was the girl's name who had gotten saved at Subway. She wanted to elaborate on what Jesus had done in her life. She said, "A few months before I met you, I had a dream and you were in it preaching the Gospel to me. When you walked into the restaurant that night and started ministering to me, I knew Jesus was real. I no longer pray to Buddha, *only Jesus!*" After hanging up the phone, I felt the Lord speak to me very promptly. He said, "I'm giving people dreams and preparing people all over America. I'm doing My job—you tell the church to do theirs. Ask them, 'Where are the deliverers?'"

It Is the Power of God

Oftentimes, the power of simply proclaiming God's Word through preaching the Gospel is overlooked. When, in fact, there is wonder-working power and supernatural activity that takes place when we proclaim the Good News. Whenever we quote, preach, minister, or mention scripture when witnessing, it releases God's power, whether we see it or not. As Paul testified, *"I am not ashamed of the gospel, because it is the power of God that brings salvation to everyone who believes"* (Rom. 1:16).

> The simple fact is that when you preach, witness, declare, or softly speak to someone one on one or in a stadium crusade, Jesus will manifest in what you claim He will do as long as it aligns with His written Word.

Romans 1:16 is one of my favorite scriptures. I love how evangelist Reinhard Bonnke makes preaching, and the manifestation of Christ that takes place through the preached word, very easy to understand. Paraphrasing, he says, "Jesus will be whatever you preach Him to be! If you preach a saving Jesus, Jesus will save. If you preach a healing Jesus, Jesus will heal. If you preach a delivering Jesus, Jesus will deliver." The simple fact is that when you preach, witness, declare, or softly speak to someone one on one or in a stadium crusade, Jesus will manifest in what you claim He will do as long as it aligns with His written Word.

We must always be ready to give an account of the Gospel! It is my conviction that everyone needs to be ready with a

30-second message to preach or declare Jesus publicly. You never know when God will need you, so we must be ready. *"Preach the word; be prepared in season and out of season; correct, rebuke and encourage—with great patience and careful instruction"* (2 Tim. 4:2). Do your best to present yourself to God as one approved, a worker who does not need to be ashamed and who correctly handles the word of truth (see 2 Tim. 2:15). You may think or believe that because you're not a pastor or evangelist this doesn't apply to you, but Jesus made no distinction. He was speaking to all believers. I want to challenge you to get a 30-second message prepared and then see if God won't have you stand and deliver it at some point. Here's mine (feel free to copy it and make it yours. Notice, I want to grab the attention of the listeners with a good opener):

> Behold the Lamb of God who takes away the sin of the world! Jesus didn't come into the world to condemn the world, but to save the world! Jesus didn't die on the cross to send you to hell, but to send you to heaven. He's not mad at you; He loves you. But the Bible says in Romans 6:23 that, *"The wages of sin is death."* So if you die in your sin, you'll go to a real hell. If you die living a life of immorality, addiction, rebellion, lying, or whatever else is contrary to God's Word concerning a life of sin, you won't make heaven. But that's not God's plan for your life. The Bible also says, "The gift of God is eternal life." Therefore, God's heart is to give you the gift of everlasting life. He wants to redeem you and set you free. So I implore you, by God's grace, turn from your sin and repent. Come to Christ and He will set you free. He loves you

and wants a relationship with you, so give Him a chance. If you move toward Him, He will run toward you.

While serving as an evangelism director at a church in the Atlanta Metro area, I was set to lead an outreach one particular night. I felt like we should go to the adult entertainment club that was nearby. We could stand outside the bar and proclaim a life-giving word that leads people to faith and repentance like the sermon I just wrote above. When I arrived at the church there were only three people who showed up—two 65-year-olds and a 67-year-old. I was frustrated. The church ran about 300 people, and when we had a guest speaker the room was full. But when I would lead an outreach to share Christ, not many would show up. If we are ever going to have an awakening, we must have a deeper burden for the lost than we do catching another renewal service for another touch. I wholeheartedly believe in renewal services, but it's way too imbalanced when it comes to reaching the community.

> If we are ever going to have an awakening, we must have a deeper burden for the lost than we do catching another renewal service for another touch.

With that being said, I thought when I told them where I felt we should go that they were going to say, "You're crazy and we're not going." I would've gone back home with a latte. However, to my surprise, they said it sounded great and were ready to go. I told them I would preach and they would pray as people entered the establishment. They felt it was a great idea.

When we arrived, we stood on a sidewalk about 200 feet from the club. I gave a 30-second message as people walked in and out of the bar. The Gospel is the power of God unto salvation, and as we preach it in faith it works. After one of the 30-second messages, a guy walked in the bar and then came out of the bar. So I gave him another 30-second shot. This happened around three to seven times. We thought it was quite wild. He heard my message several times. The last time he walked out, he jumped back into his El Camino and drove straight to us. I assumed he wanted to fight because of how he literally raced right to us. I walked over to the car and he stuck out a wad of money from the window and said, "Take this!" I replied, "I can't take that!" He said, "I insist!" So I said, "Okay." It was 36 bucks.

Then he got out of his car and said, "I'm a backslidden evangelist with a call of God on my life. The last time I walked into that bar, I got up on a stool and preached the Gospel. I told everyone about their need for Christ." Then he got down on his knees and literally put his face in the dirt weeping in repentance as he gave his heart back to Christ.

> It's not about our charisma, personality, or ability to speak. It's about how available we are for God to use us.

Why did God do this? Because I'm a good preacher? Because I've gone to Bible school? Was it because I'm a good communicator? *No!* It was none of the above. It's because I was *available* to speak God's Word. It's not about our charisma, personality, or ability to speak. It's about how available we are for God to *use* us. If it were about our personality, charisma, or vast knowledge of the Word of God, then it has everything to do with us and not much to do with God. He's not looking for the most talented, gifted, or best communicator. He's looking for someone who's available. If it were about us and we could do it alone, we wouldn't need His Word or the cross. The cross is the crux of the Gospel by which men can be saved. I love what the Bible says about the apostles: *"When they saw the courage of Peter and John and realized that they were unschooled, ordinary men, they were astonished and they took note that these men had been with Jesus"* (Acts 4:13). He will take your inability and turn it into gold if you give Him your *availability* to speak His Word and say what He is saying. Reinhard Bonnke says (paraphrasing), "I am a zero, but I'm standing next to number one! So this automatically makes me a 10!" This should be our mindset. Not our ability, but His through us.

There is irresistible power for the believer who will make him- or herself available to declare God's Word! In any form or fashion, whether preaching from the pulpit of a church, street preaching, or gently whispering God's Word to the clerk at a library, the Word has wonder-working, heart-penetrating power.

> *For the word of God is alive and active. Sharper than any double-edged sword, it penetrates even to dividing soul and spirit, joints and marrow; it judges the thoughts and attitudes of the heart* (Hebrews 4:12).

God's Word is life! When we minister it, by its very nature it brings life! It is the method in which man will be saved. *"How, then, can they call on the one they have not believed in? And how can they believe in the one of whom they have not heard? And how can they hear without someone preaching to them? And how can anyone preach unless they are sent? As it is written: 'How beautiful are the feet of those who bring good news!'"* (Rom. 10:14-15). This is very clear. We must share, preach, or declare the Gospel. In whatever form or fashion best fits your personality, we must do it. No one is exempt.

There is incredible power in the Gospel, but not if it is muted—it must be spoken by the believer:

> *For the message of the cross is foolishness to those who are perishing, but to us who are being saved it is the power of God. For it is written: "I will destroy the wisdom of the wise; the intelligence of the intelligent I will frustrate." Where is the wise person? Where is the teacher of the law? Where is the philosopher of this age? Has not God made foolish the wisdom of the world? For since in the wisdom of God the world through its wisdom did not know him, God was pleased through the foolishness of what was preached to save those who believe. Jews demand signs and Greeks look for wisdom, but **we preach** Christ crucified: a stumbling block to Jews and foolishness to Gentiles, but to those whom God has called, both Jews and Greeks, Christ the power of God and the wisdom of God. For the foolishness of God is wiser than human wisdom, and the weakness of God is stronger than human strength* (1 Corinthians 1:18-25).

> Our actions give us credibility *for the message we relate*. If Jesus didn't communicate the Gospel by His actions alone, why would we ever think we could? He was perfect for 30 years and didn't have a large following until He opened His mouth and began His preaching ministry.

Some say, "I let my actions preach the Gospel." Well, our actions give us credibility *for the message we relate*. There is *no* saving power by living a good life alone. Buddhist monks can do that, and they have zero power to save. I love and hate the statement of St. Francis of Assisi, "In all your actions preach the gospel, and if necessary use words." Without realizing it, many use that as a cop-out. It takes *words* for people to understand the Gospel. If Jesus didn't communicate the Gospel by His actions alone, why would we ever think we could? Especially if Jesus was perfect in all His actions and we will never be. He used *words* throughout His whole ministry. He was perfect for 30 years and didn't have a large following until He opened His mouth and began His preaching ministry.

Peter used words, the apostle Paul used words, John the Baptist used words, to name a few. We must use words for men and women to understand and be saved; the Bible is crystal clear on this point!

One Moment/One Sentence

When I was around 13 years old, I would attend a youth group at a charismatic church now and then. I went probably 10 to 15 times, and went for two main reasons: the pizza and the girls. I don't really remember anything the youth pastor ever preached, except on one particular night. *"So, because you are lukewarm—neither hot nor cold—I am about to spit you out of my mouth"* (Rev. 3:16). That verse never left me. I didn't go home and memorize it. I didn't make a mental note that I needed to listen carefully this particular night. I didn't really like preaching at all. But that verse stuck with me until I got saved and was a real part of my coming to Christ. Every time I would try and justify that I was saved, the Holy Spirit would whisper to me, *"You've got to be hot or cold, and if you're lukewarm I'll spit you out of My mouth."* That word spoken was a seed that gave the Holy Spirit something to work with. This verse working in my life is further proof that it's the Gospel that is power unto salvation. If I'd never heard this verse, who knows where I'd be today. How many people do you come in contact with who have never heard? And where will they be if you leave it to someone else? Sow the Word, that's all you're responsible for.

Cut to the Heart

When the people heard this, they were cut to the heart and said to Peter and the other apostles, "Brothers, what shall we do?" Peter replied, "Repent and be baptized, every one of you, in the name of Jesus Christ for the forgiveness of your sins. And you will receive the gift of the Holy Spirit. The promise is for you and your children and for all who are far off—for all whom the Lord our God will call." With many other words he warned them; and he pleaded with them, "Save yourselves from this corrupt generation."

Those who accepted his message were baptized, and about three thousand were added to their number that day (Acts 2:37-41).

They were cut to the heart by the preaching of the Gospel. What did Peter preach? In Acts 2:22–36, Peter emphasized the pure Gospel. His main points still have the power to save, heal, deliver, and free everyone from anything. His three main points began with the death of Jesus Christ. Peter strongly emphasized the great sacrifice that Jesus made on the cross. Without the cross there wouldn't have been any sin offering to cleanse us from our sin. He emphasized the resurrection—how God raised Jesus from the dead. If there wasn't a resurrection, there would have been no salvation. Over and over the apostles hammered the resurrection. He then declared the ascension.

> Are people cut so deep to the heart by your witness, preaching, or life that they ask what they can do to be saved?

After presenting the Gospel, Peter then told them to repent of their sins. He pleaded with them concerning this. We must plead and persuade people in this day as well. He didn't sugarcoat it. They were cut to the heart. This is a very challenging passage to every preacher as well as every Christian. Are people cut so deep to the heart by your witness, preaching, or life that they ask what they can do to be saved? Peter presents to the body of Christ a display of anointing and power preaching that few walk in today. God, baptize us with a fresh baptism of fire to preach in this manner to cut a lost and dying world straight to the heart until they cry, "What must we do to be saved?"

Peter called them to repent, which is a response to the Gospel, but not the Gospel itself. Monks can call people to morality and pure ethics. However, this does not save. I have heard preachers call people to repentance without preaching the Gospel. If someone doesn't understand who they are turning to and what the cross really means, it can lead to a false finish line where they never receive the transforming power of a regenerated life. So we must preach the cross, blood, resurrection, and ascension, then call people to repent of their sin and follow Christ. This is a proper response to the Gospel. It is the Gospel that cut those listening straight to the heart and 3,000 came to Christ. Do it again through our preaching of the cross, sweet Jesus!

Proclaiming the Resurrection

They were greatly disturbed because the apostles were teaching the people, proclaiming in Jesus the resurrection of the dead (Acts 4:2).

With great power the apostles continued to testify to the resurrection of the Lord Jesus. And God's grace was so powerfully at work in them all (Acts 4:33).

Or these who are here should state what crime they found in me when I stood before the Sanhedrin— unless it was this one thing I shouted as I stood in their presence: "It is concerning the resurrection of the dead that I am on trial before you today" (Acts 24:20-21).

These notable apostles of the book of Acts greatly challenge us today. They were preaching a simple theme through
and through—Christ raised from the dead. They were imprisoned for preaching this message and not because of any crime.
I've never gone to a city and preached the Gospel and resurrection so powerfully that I was imprisoned. I've never preached
in such a way that my preaching shook the entire region. How
about you? Here's what they commanded them to do concerning their preaching and the description of the impact of their
simple message:

> *Then they called them in again and commanded
> them not to speak or teach at all in the name of Jesus*
> (Acts 4:18).

> *But other Jews were jealous; so they rounded up some
> bad characters from the marketplace, formed a mob
> and started a riot in the city. They rushed to Jason's
> house in search of Paul and Silas in order to bring
> them out to the crowd. But when they did not find
> them, they dragged Jason and some other believers
> before the city officials, shouting: "These men who
> have caused trouble all over the world have now
> come here, and Jason has welcomed them into his
> house. They are all defying Caesar's decrees, saying
> that there is another king, one called Jesus"* (Acts
> 17:5-7).

> *"We gave you strict orders not to teach in this name,"*
> he said. *"Yet you have filled Jerusalem with your
> teaching and are determined to make us guilty of
> this man's blood"* (Acts 5:28).

I've never filled an entire city with the doctrine of Christ. I've never been accused of causing trouble all over the world because of my preaching. I've never been ordered not to preach in His name any longer. This convicts me. This should convict us all. The bar Christ and the apostles set was to shake cities, nations, and the world. We should make an impact that shakes the gates of hell.

> *Philip went down to a city in Samaria and pro-claimed the Messiah there. When the crowds heard Philip and saw the signs he performed, they all paid close attention to what he said. For with shrieks, impure spirits came out of many, and many who were paralyzed or lame were healed. So there was great joy in that city* (Acts 8:5-8).

How are we ever going to shake our cities if our churches aren't mobilized and equipped with the Gospel to hit the streets and believe for miracles? Now is the time and this is the season. If not now, when? If not you, who?

Our Responsibility, Their Responsibility, and God's Responsibility

> *Jonah obeyed the word of the Lord and went to Nineveh. Now Nineveh was a very large city; it took three days to go through it. Jonah began by going a day's journey into the city, proclaiming, "Forty more days and Nineveh will be overthrown." The Ninevites believed God. A fast was proclaimed, and all of them, from the greatest to the least, put on sackcloth.*

...When God saw what they did and how they turned from their evil ways, he relented and did not bring on them the destruction he had threatened (Jonah 3:3-5,10).

The simplicity of this passage is that Jonah obeyed God and preached the word of the Lord in Nineveh. Jonah had one responsibility: to preach the word. It wasn't for him to gauge his success on whether or not they heeded his word. He was successful because he obeyed and stepped out. At the end of every Gospel, in one form or fashion, we are commissioned to preach the word. Are you successful in your simple obedience in this regard?

They received the word. They took responsibility for what they heard and responded in repentance. After Jonah fulfilled his responsibility, the Ninevites also fulfilled theirs and God was faithful to withhold judgment. No matter how people respond to our message, we are still called to deliver it.

If he did not spare the ancient world when he brought the flood on its ungodly people, but protected Noah, a preacher of righteousness, and seven others (2 Peter 2:5).

We see that Noah was a preacher of righteousness, yet no one listened. No one repented of their sins. Noah preached and preached. But because no one turned to God, He destroyed them all. Was Noah a failure? By no means! He did his part; yet the people did not do theirs. Likewise, God did His part and destroyed them all.

Who was a greater success, Noah or Jonah? They both were successful because they obeyed God in preaching His Word. Jonah definitely needed a little more motivation than Noah, but in the end they both fulfilled what God requested of them. We can't hang our hat on the responses we receive but on our obedience. We're not told to proclaim the Gospel based on results but on obedience. When we do our part, God will do His, and we will see the fruit of our labor in the Name of Jesus.

Who was a greater success, Noah or Jonah? They both were successful because they obeyed God in preaching His Word.

Let's be encouraged by what God did and continues to do. Now let's take a moment to ask God to increase our hunger and to put us on the line for God's use.

> *God, help us as we put ourselves in a position to be used of You. Use me in power, Jesus, and cause me not to settle for anything less than Your supernatural manifestations. Use me, Lamb of God, to cut people to the heart as I witness, preach, and minister the resurrection of who You are and what You did.*

Take a moment and wait on God to give you a fresh anointing to preach the Gospel.

> *"Now, Lord, consider their threats and enable your servants to speak your word with great boldness. Stretch out your hand to heal and perform signs and wonders through the name of your holy servant Jesus." After they prayed, the place where they were meeting was shaken. And they were all filled with the*

Holy Spirit and spoke the word of God boldly (Acts 4:29-31).

The Power of the Seed

Many nations that were once powerful in stature concerning the Gospel and Christianity have plateaued or are in a state of decline. They have become totally secular and post-Christian. You can find a common thread in this staggering fact: the church, for the most part, quit sowing the Gospel through outreach and equipping their people to share Christ. *Somewhere along the line, the church became a maintenance department instead of a mobilized sales force.*

> Somewhere along the line, the church became a maintenance department instead of a mobilized sales force.

Imagine if a local car dealership in your area, such as Ford, Chevrolet, Toyota, or Infiniti, made a shift in policy concerning their sales force. One day the CEO of the dealership walks in and says the following to his staff: "I've been looking at the flow of finances in our dealership. The last quarter we attained more of a net profit from our maintenance department than we did from our sales force. We have a three-week wait right now on all of our maintenance work. It's amazing! The average wait time in our city at every other dealership is six hours. We are going to make a drastic shift today. We are cutting our sales force by 95 percent. If you're in sales we will gladly train you to become a mechanic and you will be able to keep a job. If you don't wish to do this, let me know by tomorrow. If this is not a fit for you, tomorrow will be your last day. We are going all in with our maintenance department. I will stay in the office and handle all of the sales when people walk in. If they really want a car, they will come in and find me. I will hire one assistant position to help me. In addition, we aren't going to advertise our product any longer. All of our resources are going into new mechanical equipment. Let's go for it!"

How long do you think it would take before they go out of business? No sales force to educate the customer on who they are and what sets their vehicles apart from the rest. No one to take the time to describe how the cars and their accessories operate. No one to just give a smile and let them know how happy they are that they stopped by to take a look. You know the answer. They might as well plan their last day now.

> When every other event the local church does (including clean-up day) is better attended than reaching lost souls, something is out of balance and needs to change.

All too often, this is the face of the church in many post-Christian nations—the ones that have plateaued or are in decline. There is an overwhelming imbalance of maintaining versus selling. There is a large imbalance in discipleship, fellowship, and Christian-centered activities versus reaching the lost through outreach and evangelism. I am by no means pitting discipleship against evangelism, but I am saying we are way out of balance in the majority of cases. *When every other event the local church does (including clean-up day) is better attended than reaching lost souls, something is out of balance and needs to change.*

Some say it's not their calling to reach people or evangelize. Some never verbalize it with words, but their actions shout it from the rooftops. James said your faith is proven by your actions (see James 2:17). What are your actions revealing about your faith? What are your actions revealing about your belief in God's power to save? Wrongly believing that you're not called to reach the lost has got to change. Put your hand to the plow, read the Word, pray, and listen for the call—the call of those perishing without a savior. Listen for the call of fathers and mothers in hell crying out for someone to please tell their sons and daughters about Jesus. The call of the multitudes who followed false religions and are now suffering in hell crying out to us to share the Gospel with their Muslim, Hindu, or Buddhist loved ones. The call of every witch who was deceived by the devil to lift your voice. Can you hear the call of the drug addict begging for freedom? The call of the cutter for whom the pain is so much that they're going to kill themselves if something doesn't happen soon? The call of Christ as He bled to death on the cross and paved the way that none should perish but all have eternal life? Can you hear it now?

To stay with the theme of a sales force, I have a scenario for you. How long do you think a salesman for a Fortune 500 company, such as Boeing, would last if he or she didn't know their product? And when they sat down with the executive team of American Airlines to close a deal, they were clueless? It wouldn't be tolerated. Their job would be terminated.

Imagine if your residence caught on fire and you called the fire department and they showed up in minutes. You were incredibly happy and just knew the damage would be very minimal as you saw three trucks and 12 strong men jump off all suited up and ready to go. Then the chief walked up and said they had a small problem. They don't have any hoses on these trucks. These were the trucks that aren't fully equipped. You would be beside yourself, furious, watching all your belongings and residence burn to the ground.

When I travel, I share this analogy and then ask the congregation a question in humility for illumination and revelation purposes only. The question is, "How many of you can give 10 scriptures, chapter and verse, on how to communicate the doctrine of Christ to an unbeliever to make the Gospel clear to them?" I think this should be the first process of all discipleship above anything else. Even for the new convert, to know what they believe and why. Then, they should know how to communicate by memory that very doctrine. If you don't know any by memory, it will hurt your effectiveness.

I would love to say that 50 percent of churches I've been to can do this. It would be an upgrade to say that even 25 percent could. It's startling that only around 2 percent at best can give you 10 scriptures from memory by chapter and verse on how to communicate the doctrine of salvation to an unbeliever. I've polled thousands, and this is the sad fact. The vast majority of the church is unequipped to share the Gospel. No wonder we're in decline as a church in the United States.

The Boeing salesman would have been fired. The fire chief would have been fired. So what will Christ to do with us? Fire us?

Then he told this parable: "A man had a fig tree growing in his vineyard, and he went to look for fruit on it but did not find any. So he said to the man who took care of the vineyard, 'For three years now I've been coming to look for fruit on this fig tree and haven't found any. Cut it down! Why should it use up the soil?' 'Sir,' the man replied, 'leave it alone for one more year, and I'll dig around it and fertilize it. If it bears fruit next year, fine! If not, then cut it down'" (Luke 13:6-9).

We see in this parable that God wants us to bear fruit and is very serious about it. We also see that His heart doesn't want to cut any down and graciously extends their time. Has God been giving you extensions? If so, make Him proud and bear fruit and sow the seed of the Gospel.

> We are sharing the Father of all mankind and introducing people to their Creator. We have the **risen** Jesus to communicate. Let's learn the message and speak life into the dead places.

I will be giving you more than ten scriptures in the next chapter on how to communicate the Gospel. If you don't already know these or have gotten a little rusty, I pray you will take the ten-scripture challenge and go for it. If you do, you will have more confidence in sharing your faith than you would have ever imagined. We have something far greater than a vehicle. We are sharing the Father of all mankind and introducing people to their Creator. We have the *risen* Jesus to communicate. Let's learn the message and speak life into the dead places.

Will We Have Another Harvest?

There was a time in the United States when the majority of the population had some sort of Christian foundation. Up until 1962, even if someone's family didn't go to church, prayer and the Word of God were a part of the educational system. There was a teacher or principal who would have shared the Gospel at some point, daily scripture reading was a part of morning announcements, a counselor often used God's Word to solve problems, or the Lord's Prayer was recited. It was seed that was planted in the hearts of an entire generation.

This made the potential for conviction a part of the moral fiber of America. When this was outlawed, we watched a major moral shift take place from one generation to the next. In 1959, a major magazine for young ladies had an article written by a teenage girl. She was expressing her brokenness from losing her virginity. Today, that same magazine wouldn't even consider an article like that. Instead it's filled with lascivious dress and sexuality. The reason for the girl writing the article in 1959 wasn't condemnation but conviction. Without godly seed, there is no conviction and you have a moral collapse because the compass is broken.

In the 1960s and '70s, if a woman got pregnant outside of wedlock, our society didn't celebrate it or accept it as the norm. They did the direct opposite. They hid it at all costs because of the conviction they felt. They would buy larger and larger shirts until they couldn't hide it any longer and had to come out with the truth of their pregnancy. Today, there's little to no conviction about it and if someone says the contrary, they're not being loving. Ladies no longer hide getting pregnant, but post it on social media and throw a party for all to come. Not that having a child isn't a time of celebration, but the way it came about has become normalized in our culture. In the 1990s, the gay culture operated in secret for the vast majority. Why? Because there was still a strong societal conviction that it was sin and God disapproved. There was still conviction. The tide has turned today and they now have parades in the streets with gross acts of lasciviousness for all to see. Why? No conviction.

There was a time when a drunk sailor fresh off the boat from decades past could give the foundations of what salvation is, who Jesus is, and what it means to be saved. If you talked to him about repentance, he probably already had the framework in his heart and could be ready for harvest. He had seed that was not only there, but had been watered over the years. He just might be ready for harvest. But in today's culture, he wouldn't be near ready outside of the miraculous because you can't harvest without seed. The conversation wouldn't be about him giving his heart to Christ, but maybe just telling who Jesus is for the first time in his life. The vast majority of people don't get saved the first time they hear the Gospel; it's over a series of touches from lay Christians and preachers.

What has caused this moral decline? Could it be that the church has for the most part ceased to sow the pure Gospel of Jesus Christ, both one on one and through mass outreaches?

My conclusion is that it's not time for a harvest, although we are in dire need of one. On the contrary, it's time to sow. You cannot reap where you have not sown. It is a spiritual principle..

Imagine a farmer whose main crop is corn decides to go on an extended vacation during spring, which is when you sow for this particular crop. He stays away for around six months, returns, gets on his combine, and expects to harvest. Everyone with common sense would tell him he's lost his mind. You can't harvest where you have not sown. It's the same reality with the Gospel. We can't expect a harvest when there isn't any fresh seed.

> It's not time for a harvest, although we are in dire need of one. On the contrary, it's time to sow. You cannot reap where you have not sown.

I believe we've reaped all we are going to from the past generation. *I wish I could say it's harvest time, but it's not.* It's time to sow! But the good news is that you can't have seasons of sacrificial sowing without a harvest springing up. There's a time to reap and a time to sow. It's time to sow!

However, I want to be clear as you read through the majority of this book—God can and will perform miracle harvests with displays of power, like in John 4 and throughout the book of Acts and the Gospels. We should always believe for the miracle harvest but not neglect sowing and not grow weary as we sow and water along the way.

The Process

Oftentimes, the "suddenly" comes at the end of an extensive process. Matthew 14 is an example. As the disciples struggled all night and feared for their lives, Jesus suddenly showed up and saved them. Lazarus was dead four days with his family feeling tremendous loss, and suddenly he was raised from the dead. The

Israelites wandered in the desert 40 years and suddenly entered the promised land. A *suddenly* happens at once after a long process. So never minimize the process of sowing the seed of the Gospel.

My wife's birthday falls on New Year's Eve. During our first year of marriage, we spent Christmas in Mobile, Alabama with my parents. So for my wife's birthday, I took her to very nice hotel in Fairhope, Alabama that overlooks Mobile Bay.

They have a nice gazebo area with fire pits, nice patio furniture, and flat screens playing sports. We sat down and began to watch a football game. Shortly after sitting down, a nice-looking couple came and sat across from us. It was apparent that they both needed a relationship with Christ. They were unmarried, but were staying together in the hotel. He was drinking Jack Daniels and using profanity. With that said, it's the exact life I used to live, so I wasn't looking down on them whatsoever. I was just eager to share whatever God wanted me to share in hopes of bringing them closer to Jesus.

I asked him what he did for a living, and he said he was a professional lacrosse player and traveled extensively across America with his team. I assumed he would ask me a follow-up question and ask me what I did. He didn't at first. I was praying and asking God if He wanted me to say anything or start a conversation about Christ. I felt led to wait because I try to practice only saying what Christ is saying and only doing what Christ is doing. About an hour later, he asked me, "What do you do?" I replied, "I'm an evangelist." After I said that, I had no idea how the conversation would go. To my surprise, he got excited that I was an evangelist and, for the most part, professed to being a Christian. He went on to talk about the church he attends and how much he enjoyed it. He spoke very highly of his pastor and how they have lunch on a regular basis. I began to internally pray on what God would have me say to him. I also thought it was odd that he went to church, had a great relationship with his pastor, confessed to being a Christian, yet was sleeping with his girlfriend, drinking Jack Daniels, and using profanity.

Before I tell you what God led me to say, we have to take a look at an individual's life who professes Christ and see if they're directly and unashamedly living in sin. This is a stark contrast to the teachings of Christ and New Testament theology. Here is one foundation that Jesus laid:

"By their fruit you will recognize them. Do people pick grapes from thornbushes, or figs from thistles? Likewise, every good tree bears good fruit, but a bad tree bears bad fruit. A good tree cannot bear bad fruit, and a bad tree cannot bear good fruit. Every tree that does not bear good fruit is cut down and thrown into the fire. Thus, by their fruit you will recognize them. Not everyone who says to me, 'Lord, Lord,' will enter the kingdom of heaven, but only the one who does the will of my Father who is in heaven. Many will say to me on that day, 'Lord, Lord, did we not prophesy in your name and in your name drive out demons and in your name perform many miracles?' Then I will tell them plainly, 'I never knew you. Away from me, you evildoers!' Therefore everyone who hears these words of mine and puts them into practice is like a wise man who built his house on the rock. The rain came down, the streams rose, and the winds blew and beat against that house; yet it did

not fall, because it had its foundation on the rock. But everyone who hears these words of mine and does not put them into practice is like a foolish man who built his house on sand. The rain came down, the streams rose, and the winds blew and beat against that house, and it fell with a great crash." When Jesus had finished saying these things, the crowds were amazed at his teaching, because he taught as one who had authority, and not as their teachers of the law (Matthew 7:16-29).

Jesus demonstrates wonderful principles for walking out the Christian life. The first was that whatever kind of fruit you bear determines who you are, not just your confession. If someone's fruit is contrary to God's Word, they may be walking in deception or the God of their understanding, and not see who He really is. The second principle is that salvation is far from simply believing the right doctrine. This is paramount to our salvation, yes. But we must also apply it to our lives. For example, if someone believes they can live a sinful lifestyle or that they can get to heaven through an avenue outside of Jesus, they are deceived. To sum it up, you must have a real change beyond a simple confession that bears witness of the confession. Third, He demonstrates that you must apply the full counsel of God. We cannot choose parts of the Bible we believe and ignore scriptures we don't like. All three outcomes of those described in the passage above who did not follow His teachings ended with destruction and hell. This, too, is a part of the Gospel that must be shared. Of course, there's a big difference between a loving warning and condemning judgment.

Then I beg you, father, send Lazarus to my family, for I have five brothers. Let him warn them, so that they will not also come to this place of torment (Luke 16:27-28).

With this passage in mind, I felt led to sow a seed of warning and not judgment. There is a big difference between condemning judgment and a heartfelt warning. Many will spin a warning into self-righteous judgment. So the question is what is real love, making someone feel okay in their sin or warning them of the consequences according to God's Word? The elephant in the room is Romans 6:23, *"The wages of sin is death."* It *must* be shared. It must be shared *in love!*

The elephant in the room is Romans 6:23, *"The wages of sin is death."* It **must** be shared. It must be shared **in love!**

Imagine being at a beautiful park such as Yellowstone with scenic picnic areas and nature trails galore. If I were on a trail to a beautiful picnic area and saw a mother grizzly bear with her two cubs at the break of the woods a half of a mile out, I wouldn't go any farther. I would quietly turn around and head back up the trail. If I saw a family of four headed the same direction and saw their picnic basket and said to myself, "I'd sure hate to hurt their plans. Maybe the bear will leave or someone else will warn them, but I don't want to be a part of interrupting their day with this altering news." There's not one person who would agree with me that I shouldn't warn them of impending danger. But when some warn of the danger of hell, they're called self-righteous and judgmental. I would beg to differ. Most are not judgmental but are lovingly and compassionately warning of the judgment that will come. I would argue that it's just as cruel for a Christian not to warn someone in error, especially a self-confessed Christian who thinks he or she is on the way to heaven while living a life that's in direct opposition to God's Word.

Here's what God led me to say to the man in Fairhope. I told him that my wife and I didn't have sex until we got married. As you know, that's not a statement you use every day with someone you've never met before. He communicated that he felt that was one of the hardest things to do these days. I then quoted and explained what the Bible says concerning sex outside of marriage.

> Or do you not know that wrongdoers will not inherit the kingdom of God? Do not be deceived: Neither the sexually immoral nor idolaters nor adulterers nor men who have sex with men nor thieves nor the greedy nor drunkards nor slanderers nor swindlers will inherit the kingdom of God (1 Corinthians 6:9-10).

It's clear from this passage that confessing Christians who live this way are deceived, as this man was. The simple definition for *deceive* is to mislead or falsely persuade others, to practice deceit. Our battle is not against flesh and blood but the devil, so the author behind this deception is the devil himself. Therefore, we must warn people who are walking in deception. Our goal is to lead people in the right direction.

I said all of this in love. I told him the next time he's with his pastor to have a Bible study on First Corinthians 6:9-10, and that was it. I didn't try to lead him to Christ. That's all I felt God wanted me to give him. I was sowing and watering. I didn't feel it was harvest time. I did my job. I lovingly and graciously warned him and gave the Holy Spirit something to use to work and convict him with.

> Our battle is not against flesh and blood but the devil, so the author behind this deception is the devil himself. Therefore, we must warn people who are walking in deception. Our goal is to lead people in the right direction.

I planted the seed, Apollos watered it, but God has been making it grow. So neither the one who plants nor the one who waters is anything, but only God, who makes things grow. The one who plants and the one who waters have one purpose, and they will each be rewarded according to their own labor. For we are co-workers in God's service; you are God's field, God's building (1 Corinthians 3:6-9).

You can never underestimate the power of a seed sown. We have to pray and determine where we are in the process. Are we sowing brand new seed? Are we watering seed that has already been sown? Has the seed sprung forth and ready to be harvested? When we sow the seed of the Gospel, it is in itself very valuable. You can't have a harvest without the seed. So every time you have the opportunity to sow the Word, do so.

God, I ask You to grant me boldness to proclaim Your Word. Give me a resolve that when I proclaim it, fruit will come forth, whether seen by me or not. I confess that You have not given me a spirit of fear, but of power. I decree that I will walk in the bold power of God as I proclaim Your Word, whether it be with a soft or loud voice. Whether it's with a coworker, classmate, family member, or a complete stranger, give me boldness to proclaim Your Gospel in the power and might of the Holy Spirit. Amen.

Chapter 10

THE MATCHLESS MESSAGE

Even though we are not always able to share the Gospel message with someone, we must be prepared to do so with each person we engage in conversation. There are times when you build a relationship and pray God will open a door. You should not feel like you have to give someone the four spiritual laws or talk about eternity the first time you meet, *especially* if it is someone you will be in contact with more than once. Neighbors, co-workers, classmates, or family members are examples of people you build relationships with and pray God opens a door for you to share the Gospel.

This reminds me of an individual my wife recently ministered to. She had been walking with one of our neighbors for around a year. She was building a relationship with her and praying that God would open a door. The lady (who we will call Cindy) is a nurse practitioner with an autoimmune disease that causes various problems. For her, it was crippling arthritis in her hands. Her Muslim fiancé was having to take care of her because her mobility was impaired significantly. She was becoming unable to perform basic functions in life and was only in her mid-30s.

My wife Trisha saw this as an open door and prayed for her to be healed. That evening, after a month of pain and immobility, she was healed. It was a real miracle. Soon afterward, her Muslim fiancé wanted to meet us and take us out for dinner. He opened the door wide, asking me about my beliefs. At that point, I shared the Gospel with them. The healing opened an opportunity for the message. The healing was not the message all by itself. It needed to be accompanied with the full Gospel message of Jesus Christ. That is why it is very important we are prepared at all times with what to say concerning the saving message of Jesus Christ, which is the Gospel—the matchless message.

Being Prepared

If we are going to sow or water the seed of the Gospel, we must have a basic foundation of scripture ready to recite at all times. We must be prepared. Looking back to the foundation is a good place to start, especially where we are as a nation at this point in our history.

It would do us well to look at the first message that was preached and take a few key points to be able to explain the foundation of salvation and how to get to saving faith. Peter preached the first Gospel message that had power to redeem people from their sins. The blood of bulls and goats did not have the power to save. Ever since sin had entered the earth there was a plan set in motion to deal with it.

> Man wasn't created to die or
> live in separation from God, so
> it had to be dealt with.

Man wasn't created to die or live in separation from God, so it had to be dealt with. When Adam and Eve sinned, it put them in a place they had never been in before—separated from God (see Gen. 3:21–24).

With this being the case, a plan was set in place for the Son of God to come and redeem mankind and set humankind free from the debt of sin. He would be the perfect Lamb, not deserving death but taking the punishment of death for our sin. According to Matthew 1:18–24, through the Holy Spirit Mary conceived. Joseph was visited by an angel who informed him that this child was from the Lord and not to divorce Mary or consummate the marriage until the child was born. He was told that the boy's name would be *Jesus* and He would save the world of their sins. This confirmed the prophecy of Isaiah the prophet, *"Therefore the Lord himself will give you a sign: The virgin will conceive and give birth to a son, and will call him Immanuel"* (Isa. 7:14).

According to Matthew 2:1–12, the magi (wise men) were coming through Jerusalem asking about Jesus's birth because they saw His star and had come to worship Him. This disturbed King Herod greatly. These magi wouldn't travel to this extent unless they had good reason. The king was nervous at the thought of another king rising to power and was greatly troubled.

He called together the chief priests and scribes and they read him a prophecy from Micah 5:2,4: *"But you, Bethlehem Ephrathah, though you are small among the clans of Judah, out of you will come for me one who will be ruler over Israel...He will stand and shepherd his flock in the strength of the Lord, in the majesty of the name of the Lord his God."*

Therefore, the king told the magi secretly to let him know where the baby was when they found him so that he could go and worship Him. However, King Herod wanted to kill Him out of fear and had no intention of worshiping Him. After they found Jesus and gave Him gifts and worshiped Him, they were warned in a dream not to tell King Herod about the child and took another route back.

Joseph was warned by an angel in a dream, as well, concerning the plot of King Herod and was told to go and hide in Egypt. This was to fulfill Hosea 11:1: *"When Israel was a child, I loved him, and out of Egypt I called my son."* They fled to Egypt to hide.

When King Herod found out that he had been outwitted by the magi, he was furious. He ordered that all the baby boys under the age of two be killed that were in Bethlehem and the vicinity. God provided a way of escape for Jesus. They did not return until after the death of King Herod. This was to fulfill the prophecy of Jeremiah: *"A voice is heard in Ramah, mourning and great weeping, Rachel weeping for her children and refusing to be comforted, because they are no more"* (Jer. 31:15).

The only one ever born who didn't deserve death took on death to cancel the debt of sin for mankind.

Jesus lived a perfect life. He was without sin. This was needed in order to take on the burden of sin and become the great sacrifice for the sin of the world. The only one ever born who didn't deserve death took on death to cancel the debt of sin for mankind.

> *And by that will* [of God which Christ performed], *we have been made holy through the sacrifice of the body of Jesus Christ once for all. Day after day every priest stands and performs his religious duties; again and again he offers the same sacrifices, which can never take away sins. But when this priest had offered for all time one sacrifice for sins, he sat down at the right hand of God, and since that time he waits for his enemies to be made his footstool. For by one sacrifice he has made perfect forever those who are being made holy* (Hebrews 10:10-14).

He was betrayed by Judas and condemned by Pontius Pilate (see Matt. 26:14–16; 27:24–26). He died a criminal's death. The cross was the most humiliating way to die. It was reserved for the worst of society.

The process of the cross and crucifixion was brutal. Jesus was utterly humiliated and mocked. They stripped him of His clothes and put a scarlet robe on Him; they put a crown of thorns on His head, gave Him a staff, and mocked Him by kneeling in front of Him. They cried out, "Hail, king of the Jews!" They spit on him and took the staff and hit Him in the head again and again. After they had mocked Him, they took Him away to crucify Him. It's good to know these points and exactly where it's found. This is the story of salvation and we must be able to recite it.

The cross would bring utter humiliation for the world to see. He was hung between two thieves who, along with the soldiers, hurled insults at Him. Matthew 27:45–65 tells us that around 3:00 P.M. Jesus died.

> *At that moment the curtain of the temple was torn in two from top to bottom. The earth shook, the rocks split and the tombs broke open. The bodies of many holy people who had died were raised to life. They came out of the tombs after Jesus' resurrection and went into the holy city and appeared to many people* (Matthew 27:51-53).

Jesus's body was taken and placed in a tomb. The Pharisees influenced Pilate to have the tomb guarded so His disciples wouldn't steal the body.

> *After the Sabbath, at dawn on the first day of the week, Mary Magdalene and the other Mary went to look at the tomb. There was a violent earthquake, for an angel of the Lord came down from heaven and, going to the tomb, rolled back the stone and sat on it. His appearance was like lightning, and his clothes were white as snow. The guards were so afraid of him that they shook and became like dead men. The angel said to the women, "Do not be afraid, for I know that you are looking for Jesus, who was crucified. He is not here; he has risen, just as he said. Come and see the place where he lay. Then go quickly and tell his disciples: 'He has risen from the dead and is going ahead of you into Galilee. There you will see him.' Now I have told you." So the women hurried away from the*

tomb, afraid yet filled with joy, and ran to tell his disciples. Suddenly Jesus met them. "Greetings," he said. They came to him, clasped his feet and worshiped him. Then Jesus said to them, "Do not be afraid. Go and tell my brothers to go to Galilee; there they will see me" (Matthew 28:1-10).

This is the matchless message—the death, burial, resurrection, and ascension of Jesus Christ for the redemption of mankind. This is the completed work of the cross. Now let's look at the process to bring an individual's understanding in line with the message.

Putting Seed in the Ground

The Sinful "Christian"

I have met countless numbers of people who will say they believe the very message of Christ. And because they believe it, they firmly believe that they are on their way to heaven even though their life doesn't bear fruit and they live a life of sin. As I stated in the previous chapter, this is where we must warn those who are deceived. You warn people by God's Word and by His Word alone. It's all we have to stand on.

We must believe, but belief alone will not get us to heaven, as noted by James, *"You believe that there is one God. Good! Even the demons believe that—and shudder"* (James 2:19). There must be a response to what we believe. The devil and his demons will not be redeemed, yet they firmly believe. To believe is the chief foundation in which salvation comes, but it is the beginning and not the end. *"Jesus answered, 'I am the way and the truth and the life. No one comes to the Father except through me'"* (John 14:6).

Therefore, believing that Jesus is the only way is imperative. We must believe in Him and the saving work that He did. The virgin birth, His perfect sacrifice to cover our sins, His death on the cross, the resurrection, the ascension, and that He is coming back for His bride. But believing without a response is not enough.

> ## When someone believes the Gospel there must be a response to it.

When someone believes the Gospel there must be a response to it. Peter's first message demanded a response. This was the first Gospel message ever preached with redemptive power due to the shed blood of Christ. *"Repent and be baptized, every one of you, in the name of Jesus Christ for the forgiveness of your sins"* (Acts 2:38). Peter is exhorting the people to turn from their sin. You cannot continue in the same direction when you turn. You have not truly surrendered to Christ unless you respond properly and turn from your sin.

Many will say, to deflect the conversation and to keep from having to look at themselves, "Well, no one's perfect." I have found that many who say this, more often than not, are living in sin and have never really surrendered their lives to Christ and taken up their cross to follow Christ.

> *This is the message we have heard from him and declare to you: God is light; in him there is no darkness at all. If we claim to have fellowship with him and yet walk in the darkness, we lie and do not live out the truth. But if we walk in the light, as he is in*

*the light, we have fellowship with one another, and
the blood of Jesus, his Son, purifies us from all sin*
(1 John 1:5-7).

There is a big difference between committing a sin and walking in sin. It is clear here that if an individual is living in sin they are not in relationship with Christ, and this must be communicated to save people from deception. *"Therefore, if anyone is in Christ, the new creation has come: The old has gone, the new is here!"* (2 Cor. 5:17).

Paul is clearly indicating that when an individual truly accepts Christ the old man is dead and the new is come. We have to put the old man to death, and when the old nature tries to resurrect itself we have to die to it. Before we have new life, we have to die to the old one. So if we are still practicing sin from our old life, according to God's Word we are deceived.

*What shall we say, then? Shall we go on sinning
so that grace may increase? By no means! We are
those who have died to sin; how can we live in it any
longer? Or don't you know that all of us who were
baptized into Christ Jesus were baptized into his
death? We were therefore buried with him through
baptism into death in order that, just as Christ
was raised from the dead through the glory of the
Father, we too may live a new life. For if we have
been united with him in a death like his, we will
certainly also be united with him in a resurrection
like his. For we know that our old self was crucified
with him so that the body ruled by sin might be done
away with, that we should no longer be slaves to*

sin—because anyone who has died has been set free from sin (Romans 6:1-7).

Paul clearly tells us that grace by no means gives anyone liberty to live in sin. It's in direct opposition to the life one proclaims. If we truly received grace, we died to sin. This is the spiritual significance of water baptism. We go under and bury our old man and die, then rise up in new life with Christ. Therefore, we are totally changed and the sinful life that used to identify us is dead and the new life of Christ now identifies us. This is the fruit of our salvation. It's not earned by any stretch of the imagination. It is just lived out and the proof is a completely changed life. We are no longer slaves to sin, because if we truly died to it, we were freed from it.

The Non-Christian

Many have never heard a clear presentation of salvation and the work of Jesus Christ. Here are scriptures that bring the Gospel into a clearer path to salvation and personal application.

As it is written: "There is no one righteous, not even one" (Romans 3:10).

For all have sinned and fall short of the glory of God (Romans 3:23).

Or do you not know that wrongdoers will not inherit the kingdom of God? Do not be deceived: Neither the sexually immoral nor idolaters nor adulterers nor men who have sex with men nor thieves nor the greedy nor drunkards nor slanderers nor swindlers will inherit the kingdom of God (1 Corinthians 6:9-10).

Have you ever met an individual who said, "I'm not that bad" or "I go to church"? He or she then compares how they are not as bad as most people. The bar is not most people, preachers, or the pope—it's Jesus! He was sinless and the only one who didn't deserve death. So we must communicate what we have fallen short of. We have fallen short of the glory of God.

This should be made clear—there is nothing we can do to earn salvation. No one is good enough. There's no one who is righteous. What is the glory of God? I'm not going to try and describe His manifest glory, but some of the attributes are purity, holiness, righteousness, a sinless state, perfection, love, joy, and peace, just to name a few. So it's not a question of not falling short of most people; it's a question of not falling short of God's glory. Other than Jesus, there's no one who didn't fall short of perfection, pure holiness, one hundred percent righteousness. This creates a need for salvation and explains that no matter how good we are no one is righteous; we've all missed the bar. But wait! There's hope: *"God demonstrates his own love for us in this: While we were still sinners, Christ died for us"* (Rom. 5:8).

> No matter how good we are no one is righteous; we've all missed the bar.

No matter how we rate a certain sin, sin is sin and we need to turn from it and repent. The good news is that while we were in our sin and in direct opposition to God, He died for us. That's the greatest news that is or ever will be. Jesus died to cover our sins as reprobate sinners. That's a gracious, loving, and merciful God. We just have to accept it and turn.

Here is one of the most clear and balanced scriptures to salvation in the entire Bible: *"For the wages of sin is death, but the gift of God is eternal life in Christ Jesus our Lord"* (Rom. 6:23). Sin leads to death—not just a physical death but a spiritual death that will mean an eternity outside of the presence of God, which will be great torture ever after. But through God's grace and goodness, He provided a way of escape through the cross and gave us His Son so that we might inherit eternal life.

We have the opportunity to accept and receive this great gift and experience eternal life. *"For God so loved the world that he gave his one and only Son, that whoever believes in him shall not perish but have eternal life"* (John 3:16).

> God wants to redeem us from our sin. His heart is not to release condemnation but forgiveness. He's just waiting on our response.

Paul, in Romans 6:23, is very clear that it's not God's will that any should perish. Peter confirms this: *"The Lord is not slow in keeping his promise, as some understand slowness. Instead he is patient with you, not wanting anyone to perish, but everyone to come to repentance"* (2 Pet. 3:9). Jesus didn't die on the cross to send people to hell but to redeem man from their sin. He didn't bleed to give Himself authority to condemn the world but to save the world. *"For God did not send his Son into the world to condemn the world, but to save the world through him"* (John 3:17). God wants to redeem us from our sin. His heart is not to release condemnation but forgiveness. He's just waiting on our response.

The Great Exchange

If anyone is away from the Lord, He wants to make an exchange with that individual. He wants to take sin and give forgiveness. His heart is to take any immorality and trade it for purity. He's in the business of taking addiction and giving liberty. His heart is to take anger, rage, and violence and give peace, love, and joy. He wants to take depression and give perfect joy. He takes the sin that leads to death and gives freedom and salvation. He takes a heart corrupted by sin and leaves a clean heart in its place. He gives us a brand-new heart. That's the miracle of it all. God not only changes hearts but He gives us a new one. As Ezekiel prophesied, *"I will give you a new heart and put a new spirit in you; I will remove from you your heart of stone and give you a heart of flesh"* (Ezek. 36:26).

How does this happen?

> *If you declare with your mouth, "Jesus is Lord," and believe in your heart that God raised him from the dead, you will be saved. For it is with your heart that you believe and are justified, and it is with your mouth that you profess your faith and are saved* (Romans 10:9-10).

With the foundation being set, this is where we want to lead people. It's not just the right words repeated after a preacher to get out of hell, but a life surrendered and turned over to Christ with everything that we are. So as we declare and believe in the work of the cross from our heart, God justifies us. Then when we confess it by faith God saves us. This is the full counsel of God, not just bits and pieces. This is truly bowing to the Lordship of Christ.

It's not just the right words repeated after a preacher to get out of hell, but a life surrendered and turned over to Christ with everything that we are.

For it is by grace you have been saved, through faith—and this is not from yourselves, it is the gift of God—not by works, so that no one can boast. For we are God's handiwork, created in Christ Jesus to do good works, which God prepared in advance for us to do (Ephesians 2:8-10).

The best news is that we don't have to earn it—just submit to what He did and He gives it to us freely. Even if we were born pure and only sinned once in our lives, we still could not earn our salvation. We have to accept the work of the cross and His Lordship, and then He gives salvation to us freely. There's no works we can do; it's His gift to us. What a wonderful gift and exchange. He takes a corrupted life and saves it from sin, not on its merit but His. Now that's Good News, and no other religion in the world has that.

Conclusion

It is my prayer that you will use the tools in this book and apply them to your everyday life. Now more than ever before in the United States and around the world we need Holy Spirit-empowered believers who move in signs, wonders, and miracles. It is just as important that every believer have not just a grasp but a firm, confident grip on how to communicate the full Gospel of Jesus Christ. We can't afford to have one without the other. The Gospel is not just for salvation. We shouldn't just preach and witness with salvation being the finish line if, for example, the individual is sick. We should share the Gospel and lay hands on the sick. In the same spirit we shouldn't stop at miracles; we must also share the Gospel. Each of these were wedded partners in the patterns of the book of Acts. They never saw healing without giving the Gospel. You could receive a divine miracle and still not go to heaven without responding to the Gospel. So we must do both.

Lord, empower every reader with a fresh baptism of fire and boldness to proclaim You and demonstrate Your power. Raise up an army of fierce soul-winning and miracle-working believers. Let us never be satisfied until we are operating and walking in what You did, Jesus, as well as the early apostles. I pray that would be the bar that we set for ourselves and never stop believing until we are walking it out!

ABOUT JOE ODEN

Joe currently serves as the GO2020 National Coordinator for the Assemblies of God, the Evangelism Coordinator for the North Texas District of the Assemblies of God, and on the executive committee of Global Evangelism Alliance, a division of Empowerment 21. In addition, he serves on an Apostolic Council team, led by Cindy Jacobs.

He is the executive director of a SUM Bible College and Theological Seminary extension site in the Dallas Metroplex and has served as an adjunct professor at several different Bible Colleges, including CFNI, Heartland School of Ministry, and SUM.

Joe was saved through the Brownsville Revival, and had the opportunity to serve as Evangelist Steve Hill's Evangelism Director at Heartland World Ministries Church. Joe received his undergraduate degree at the Brownsville Revival School of Ministry and his Master of Arts in Biblical Studies at SUM Bible College and Theological Seminary.

Joe is an author of three books and has traveled America and the world for over 20 years as an evangelist to equip, ignite, and mobilize the local church for the great commission. He has also appeared on many influential Christian television programs.